Negro Freemasory and Segregation

by

Donn A. Cass

ISBN: 978-1-63923-155-3

Negro Freemasory and Segregation

Printed: November 2021

Cover Art By: Paul Amid

Published and Distributed By:

Lushena Books
607 Country Club Drive, Unit E
Bensenville, IL 60106
www.lushenabks.com

ISBN: 978-1-63923-155-3

Printed in the United States of America

NEGRO FREEMASONRY
and
SEGREGATION

Prince Hall, from an early portrait.

PREFACE

Segregation and discrimination against Negro Freemasons has been the subject of discussion and controversy for many years. Long and complicated lawsuits, filed and prosecuted by both Negro and white Lodges have occupied the public's attention, and the consequent interest has resulted in a demand for authoritative information as to the factors entering into this much-debated and as yet unsolved question.

It is the purpose of the present work to present facts of record, taken from the writings of prominent Masonic scholars and historians, archives and official publications of Grand and subordinate Lodges, together with excerpts from the works of leading Masonic authorities, and thus establish a basis for a better understanding of Negro Freemasonry and its place in the Masonic body.

A certain amount of historical background is necessary to a full understanding of this problem and is presented, necessarily in abridged form, in this work. While an attempt has been made to limit this to pertinent material, much has been included that is intended to assist in presenting an accurate picture of the over-all position of Negro Lodges and their problems in the struggle to gain the dignity and position to which their Masonic status appears to entitle them.

From a study of the original sources quoted herein, it becomes evident that the prejudice which admittedly exists against "Lodges made up of colored men, imitating and claiming to be Masons, using regalia and emblems copied from legitimate Freemasonry" (Darrah; History and Evolution of Freemasonry) is not recognized as prejudice, but is based on the assumption that Negro Masonry is spurious and illegitimate, and will so exist "as long as human prejudice separates the white man and the black man".

Donn A. Cass

August 30, 1957
Chicago, Illinois.

TABLE OF CONTENTS

APPENDIX

CHAPTER I

BIOGRAPHICAL SKETCH OF PRINCE HALL

Prince Hall was born at Bridgetown, Barbados, British West Indies. The date of his birth is generally accepted as September 12, 1748, although there is no complete agreement on this point among historians.

His father, Thomas Prince Hall, was an English leather worker, and his mother a free colored woman of French extraction. Very little is known of the circumstances of his early life, except that his parents were said to have been industrious and of good reputation.

When Hall reached the age of seventeen he decided to leave home, as the future possible in the leather trade to which he had been apprenticed was not great enough to interest him as a life work. He left Bridgetown and arranged to work his passage on a boat to Boston, where he arrived in March, 1765 and was fortunate in securing work immediately at his trade of leather work. He worked hard and saved his wages, and by the time he was twenty-five he was the owner of real estate and was qualified to vote. The census of that time lists him as a soap maker.

Hall was thrifty and industrious. He realized the handicap imposed by his lack of education, and began to study at night after work. He completed his education in this way, and became a student of the Bible, later becoming a preacher with a charge at Cambridge. Some of his sermons have been preserved, and they indicate not only his zeal and eloquence, but a steady cultural and intellectual development.

Sometime before his twenty-first year he married one Sarah Ritchery. The exact date is unknown, as is anything else about this marriage and the death of his wife, except that she died on February 26th, 1769. Hall at that time was only twenty-one, so the marriage was obviously short lived. The reverse side of Hall's own head stone at his grave shows the inscription:

HERE LIES YE BODY OF SARAH
RITCHERY WIFE OF PRINCE HALL.
DIED FEBRUARY 26TH 1769. AGED
24 YEARS.

Hall married again in his forty-sixth year. His second wife was Phoebe Baker. There is no record of issue by either marriage.

Physically, Hall is known to have been rather short, standing five feet three inches tall, slightly built and delicately formed. He was of fair complexion, with regular and refined features, and his eyes were said to be bright and piercing. Although of slight build, he was a man of considerable energy, and he engaged in hard work despite his delicate frame. He had a wide range of interests, which included government as well as religion, and worked towards his objectives vigorously and intelligently.

NEGRO FREEMASONRY AND SEGREGATION

Prince Hall appears to have been a man of exceptional intelligence, and achieved considerable prominence as a leader of Boston's colony of free colored men. His position in the Church gave him considerable prestige, which he used to further the interests of his race, and also aided him greatly in his civic activities. Contemporary historians have referred to him as "a very intelligent black man", and have mentioned him very favorably on many occasions.

As one of the first abolitionists, Hall never overlooked an opportunity to help his less fortunate colored brothers. His petitions and memorials to the Massachusetts assembly are remarkable documents, and attest clearly to the energy and intelligence which he brought to their preparation. He advocated citizenship for colored men, participation in government, and equality before the law. He was an avid protector of his people from indignity and insult, and opposed vigorously class or racial discrimination of any kind.

He petitioned the Massachusetts legislature to establish proper schools for colored children, and his efforts were of great assistance in having such a school opened in 1796, after nine years of tireless effort to that end.

Various sources state that at the outbreak of the War of the Revolution he urged the enlistment of slaves, and addressed Hancock and Warren, who were members of the Committee of Safety, to further this move. If adopted this would have been one great step to freedom and Hall realized this. The Committee, however, decided against the proposal, but did not oppose the enlistment of freemen. Hall is said to have led a delegation of his Lodge members to call on General Washington on this same matter. Whether as a direct result of Hall's actions or otherwise, the General did issue an order permitting the enlistment of freeman. Approximately five thousand colored men served in the Revolutionary Army, even though the order permitting their enlistment was rescinded one year later. It is certain that this precedent had considerable influence on the position which Massachusetts adopted on the Negro soldier in the Civil War. While the part Hall is said to have played in this matter is not, possibly, historically proven, General Washington's correspondence and the records of the Committee of Safety give some substance to the assumption that Hall's work was of great importance in affecting this decision.

Prince Hall, probably more than any other American Mason of his time, was in close touch with the Grand Lodge of England over a period of many years. From 1784 to 1806 he was in constant communication with the secretary of the English Grand Lodge, and his letter-book, which fortunately has been preserved, contains a record in his own hand of many of these messages which he addressed to the English secretary, together with his own personal correspondence and sermons.

NEGRO FREEMASONRY AND SEGREGATION

This letter-book was discovered in 1899, together with the minutes of African Lodge No. 1 in the possession of members of the John T. Hilton Lodge of Lynn, Massachusetts. It had been damaged by water and smoke in the 1869 fire which destroyed the Temple as well as some of the records of Prince Hall Grand Lodge. Parts of the book were well preserved, but the ink on some pages was bleached and illegible.

While the character of the letter-book indicates the methodical mind and the business-like manner in which Hall conducted his correspondence and kept his records, it seems probable that not all of the letters were copied immediately upon being written—in some cases dates are at variance, and in others the copy written by Hall in his book does not agree in every detail with the wording of the original documents. The only correspondence between Masons in Boston, or, for that matter, in the United States with the Grand Lodge of England appears to be that carried on by Hall. William White, the English Grand Secretary, seems to have had no American Masonic contacts nor to have known of any since 1770 except with the African Lodge. Hall's records show that African Lodge contributed to the Grand Charity Fund, and that members of his Lodge were fraternally received by the English, and also that the parent Grand Lodge had attemped to secure through Hall information about subordinate Lodges in Boston with which any form of contact had been lost.

NEGRO FREEMASONRY AND SEGREGATION

The letter-book also records copies of addresses made by Hall on St. John's Day, and indicates that copies were sent to the English Grand Secretary, who acknowledged them with commendation. It records the payment of fees to the Grand Lodge of England, and shows that the English body transmitted printed copies of their proceedings for the information of African Lodge No. 1. This remarkable document clearly indicates how seriously Hall took his Masonic duties, and the scrupulous attention he paid to the keeping of his records in proper order.

Hall served in the Revolutionary Army, enlisting in February, 1776. He served in Captain Benjamin Dillingham's Company, in Captain Joshua Welboro's Company, and in Thacker's Regiment. His enlistment was permitted by the same order of General Washington, later rescinded, which allowed freemen to serve, and which he himself had been instrumental in initiating. While details of his Army career are lacking, he appears to have served with honor.

After his release from his brief Army service, Prince Hall devoted himself principally to civic and Masonic work, and continued to press for the best interests of his race. He continued his anti-slavery activities and in 1777 with some others addressed a petition to the legislature protesting against slavery in the colony. He also protested against the kidnapping and sale into slavery of Negroes who had been taken from Boston by force in a sailing ship. The

NEGRO FREEMASONRY AND SEGREGATION

result of his effort was that the men were returned to Boston and released. This petition was dated February 27, 1788.

He continued his works of charity and benevolence until his death on December 4, 1807 of pneumonia after a month's illness. He was buried in the historic Copps Hill Cemetery in Boston, and on June 25, 1895 a fine monument was unveiled over his grave. Many representatives of Grand Lodges of the United States attended, and representatives of foreign countries were present. The dedication concluded with a procession reviewed by the Governor of Massachusetts and other dignitaries, and was followed by a banquet at historic Faneuil Hall.

Prince Hall, eighty-eight years after his death, was fittingly, although belatedly, honored.

CHAPTER II

THE EARLY HISTORY OF NEGRO FREEMASONRY

Prince Hall was the first Negro to be initiated into the Masonic Order in the United States. On March 6, 1775, Hall and fourteen other free colored men were initiated into Lodge No. 441, a British Army Lodge working under the Grand Lodge of Ireland and at that time stationed in Boston. It is very probable that Hall was initiated alone before that date; a belief held by Grimshaw and others, but the minutes of the March 6th meeting record only one initiation on that date. The regiment to which this Lodge was attached, under the command of General Gage, later moved to New York and became one of the Lodges which took part in forming the first colored Grand body there.

African Lodge No. 1 developed from this same group; although a complete and historically accurate picture of its development can be obtained only by tracing and correlating a mass of contradictory evidence and statements, the picture is sufficiently clear to show that African Lodge No. 1 was organized, first under a 'Permit' or dispensation, held meetings, applied for and received its charter, all in correct and proper legal form and according to the widespread Masonic usage of those times. This has been questioned so often that it is necessary to re-affirm it now, an affirmation which carries the weight of

NEGRO FREEMASONRY AND SEGREGATION

authority since the report "A Consideration of the Subject of Negro Freemasonry by the Most Worshipful Grand Lodge of Masons in Massachusetts at its Quarterly Communications on March 12, 1947" has been made public. This report, printed verbatim elsewhere in this work, does not support the legitimacy of other colored Lodges, but specifically states "that the so-called Prince Hall (Negro) Freemasonry is, alone, entitled to any claim of legitimacy among Negroes in this Commonwealth."

When the military Lodge which initiated Hall and his group left Boston on March 17, 1776, the Master of the Lodge, Bro. J. B. Batt issued them a "permit" or dispensation which permitted them to meet as a Lodge and to conduct certain ceremonies; to assemble in their capacity as Freemasons for the purpose of attending church and burying their dead. This "permit" was a valid legal document, issued in accordance with the well-established custom of the day. It was regular and legal in every particular and followed well-established Masonic usage. There are many parallels to this case, none of which has ever been in question. The civilian members of Union Lodge of Albany, New York (now Mt. Vernon No. 3) who were made in the Army Lodge No. 74 of Ireland, were given in 1759 when the Army Lodge left Albany, a copy of No. 74's warrant and were authorized to meet and act as a Lodge. Betoutet Lodge No. 7 (Caucasian) at Gloucester Court House, Virginia, was operating under permission granted to it by the Fredericksburg Lodge No. 4 until it obtained its own charter from a Grand Lodge in 1773.

Fredericksburg Lodge No. 4 at Fredericksburg, Virginia, also gave permission to a group of Masons to establish Falmouth Lodge in Stafford County, Virginia. These cases should certainly establish the validity and legality of the other Lodges named as operating under the same type of dispensation, and they have not been questioned, although the "permit" in the case of the Prince Hall group has been under attack many times as being spurious and illegitimate.

On the basis of the facts given above it is no longer possible to doubt the legality of the basis on which African Lodge No. 1 was established. Soon after receiving the "permit" Hall and his group petitioned Joseph Warren, who was then the Provincial Grand Master, for recognition. The petition is said to have been favorably received, but Joseph Warren was killed at the Battle of Bunker Hill before any action could be taken on it. Another application for recognition is believed to have been made in 1779, but no record available indicates that it was more productive of results than the first petition.

The exact date of organization of African Lodge No. 1 is in doubt, although both DeGrasse and Hayden state that it was upon the exact day that Washington took command of the Army at Cambridge, July 3, 1775. A letter of Prince Hall states that the organiza-

NEGRO FREEMASONRY AND SEGREGATION

tion was one year after the initiation, or in 1776, and would seem to have more value than the date given by DeGrasse, who writes that his surmise is based on Hall's letter. DeGrasse appears to have been in error by one year, and it is probable that Hayden unconsciously compounded this same error. July 3, 1776 is probably the exact date and corresponds with that given by Hall in his application to the Grand Lodge of England for a warrant, following closely on the departure of the Army Lodge from Boston, on May 1, 1776.

Records of African Lodge No. 1, dated from 1779 to 1787 have been preserved, and are of great value in establishing the fact that the lodge did meet. While these records are not formal minutes as such, they appear to be the original notes of the secretary from which the minutes were later written.

The regulations of African Lodge No. 1, dated July 14, 1779 are also important in establishing the organization and existence of the Lodge. A copy of this document is in the British Grand Lodge Library, being sent shortly after the Lodge was constituted under the charter. The by-laws of the Lodge and its roster were sent by Prince Hall to Rowland Holt, Deputy Grand Master, as required by the provisions of the charter. Hall's letter dated May 18, 1787 informed Holt of their transmission.

On March 2, 1784, Prince Hall wrote to the Grand Lodge of England, stating that "this lodge has been founded almost eight years". This interesting document continues with an application for a warrant, and since it comments upon and thanks William M. Moody, Master, for "brotherly courtesy to my Brothers Reade and Mene, when in a strange land and in a time of need, you was so good as to receive them as Brothers, and to treat them so cordially, as they informed me you did", it appears to be obvious that the Grand Lodge of England was fully aware of the fact that African Lodge No. 1 was a Negro Lodge.

Hall signed himself "Your loving friend and Brother, Prince Hall, Master of the African Lodge No. 1". Davies advances the theory that Moody did not consider this letter, in Hall's individual name, a sufficient application, and that he probably requested a more formal and official application from the Lodge. This second letter, apparently dated June 30, 1784, resulted in the granting of a charter issued on September 29, 1784, and this is recorded together with a record of the fees paid, as part of the Transactions of the Grand Lodge of England. There seem to have been no preliminary inquiries, and this would indicate that the Grand Master of England must have been fully informed about African Lodge No. 1, its status and the character of the petitioners prior to the granting of the petition and the issuance of the warrant.

The charter was not actually received by Hall until 1787, although Hall knew that it had been granted; his letter of September 22, 1785 thanking the Grand Master of England for his action in granting the charter clearly shows this.

The delay in receiving the charter was occasioned by a whole series of misadventures; Hall's messenger, Brother Gregory, had neglected to call at the London offices of the Grand Lodge to secure it; another messenger, Brother Spooner, also neglected to call for it, and finally on December 18, 1786, Hall wrote to Moody that Captain Scott would advance the money "sent by me in his ship two years ago by his steward Hartfield". On March 10, 1787, Moody wrote Hall and informed him that Captain Scott had called in person for the warrant. Captain Scott himself finally delivered it to Prince Hall on April 29, 1787. These delays resulted in various misunderstandings, and it was even charged that the charter had been lost or stolen. A reward was offered for its recovery in the Boston Sentinel, which later published the news of its receipt. Several other Colonial newspapers also published news items dealing with African Lodge No. 1 and the granting and receipt of its charter.

The delays were also responsible for the circulation of many falsehoods, industriously published by enemies of Negro Freemasonry during the early ca-

reer of African Lodge No. 1. Among the charges
made were that Captain Scott had misrepresented
the facts to the Grand Lodge of England, that the
Grand Lodge of England was not aware that African
Lodge No. 1 was composed of Negroes. These charges,
of course, were inspired by malice, as Captain Scott
had nothing to do with the Charter except to act as
messenger for Prince Hall, and in no event could have
influenced in 1787 the granting of a warrant in 1784.
Further, Hall's letter-book shows that at least four
members of African Lodge No. 1 had been in London
and had personal contact with the offices of the
Grand Lodge there. No deception could have been
practiced, nor is there any evidence that any was
contemplated.

With the receipt of the charter, African Lodge
No. 1 was constituted into African Lodge No. 459 on
May 6, 1787, with Prince Hall as Master. The receipt
of the charter and formal constitution of the Lodge
renewed interest and activity among colored Masons.
Many colored men from New England, New York and
Philadelphia as well as Boston were received into the
Lodge. None but freemen were eligible and, according
to Belknap, great care was taken to ensure that only
worthy colored men received the degrees. The reports of Prince Hall to the Grand Lodge of England
and the evidence of fees paid show that the Lodge
was prosperous and growing. The names of new

members, as given in the letter-book and in correspondence with the Grand Lodge of England also
serve to show the growing interest in the Lodge and
its increasing strength.

At the time African Lodge No. 1 was established
there were numerous white Lodges in Boston and
New England. African Lodge was openly and publicly
established, and it is interesting to note that there is
no record of any protest against it, either locally or
in England. Its legitimacy was not attacked by the
Masons of that time, nor was any charge of invasion
of jurisdiction advanced. African Lodge No. 459 was
the only Lodge in Massachusetts then holding a warrant from the Grand Lodge of England, and it appears
strange that if its legitimacy was in question at that
time no record has been preserved to so indicate.

The later career of African Lodge No. 459, however, has been the subject of much misinformation.
At the time the charter was obtained from England
and its validity established beyond question by English records, opponents of colored Masonry claimed
that the lodge had become dormant, and had subse-
quently been revived in an irregular manner, making
it and all of its descendants and successors "clandestine and illegal". These charges were obviously false
in the light of facts established relating to the organization and constituting of the Lodge, and appear to
have been circulated only to effect a slur on the
legitimacy of Negro Masons.

C. W. Moore, of the Grand Lodge of Pennsylvania is said to have been the source of this "dormancy" charge. It was claimed that African Lodge No. 459 became dormant shortly after the death of Prince Hall in 1807, and remained dormant until 1824. The record, however, indicates that this was not the case; advertisements carried regularly in the Massachusetts Register, published in Boston, include this notice from 1806 to 1813:

> "The African Lodge in Boston meets regularly at the house of Prince Hall, in Congress Street, on the evening of the first Tuesday in each month."

The roster of the Lodge from 1775 to 1809 shows an enrolled membership of 124, which included the original 15 members during those years. In 1812 or 1813 Prince Sanders was a representative of the African Lodge to the Grand Lodge of England. He was initiated in 1809 and became Secretary in 1811. Sanders was a man of remarkable intelligence, and was received both socially and fraternally in England.

There is considerably more evidence to indicate the falsity of the "dormancy" charge, and Moore of Pennsylvania was in a position to know it. In 1869 a group of colored Masons petitioned the Massachusetts Grand Lodge for recognition. Moore was a member of the committee which declined to even examine the written records and other data submitted in proper support of the petition. Those records showed the continuous existence of African Lodge No. 459 from the date of its organization, with the original minutes of the Lodge, showing that in the years between 1807 and 1846 over 450 meetings were held. They also showed that, during the period of alleged dormancy, from 1808 to 1824, degrees were conferred upon 80 candidates at 142 meetings. Jacob Norton examined the records after the committee of the Massachusetts Grand Lodge "declined" to do so, and published a description of the minute book in his "Early History of Masonry in Massachusetts."

This minute book is a valuable source of material relating to the activities and career of African Lodge No. 459 during this period, and was in the possession of Thomas Dalton, who entered African Lodge in 1825. Dalton was very active in abolition work, being President of the Massachusetts General Colored Association in 1833. He had personal knowledge of many of the persons appearing on the roster of African Lodge No. 459 both before and after his initiation, even recalling a Masonic funeral conducted in 1810.

The alleged dormancy of the Lodge was a surprise to Dalton, and when informed of the charge in 1876, when he was 83 years old, he executed an affidavit denying the dormancy completely. He affirmed that, as Keeper of the Archives of African Lodge No. 459 and having had in his possession the records of the Lodge during the period of the alleged dormancy, he knew the charge to be completely false. Dalton had signed the Declaration as Senior Warden in 1827 when he was, in his own words, "intimately acquainted with all the old members of the said Lodge, and often heard them conversing about the then existing African Lodge years before I joined it. Subsequent to my initiation, I took an interest in the affairs of the Lodge, and frequently associated with and conversed with the said brethren; often heard them relate some of the early Masonic reminiscences, but I never heard that the Lodge had ceased holding its regular meetings before I was initiated until I was informed the other day about the reports circulated to that effect in the proceedings of the Grand Lodges of the White Masons." Dalton signed this document on October 10, 1876.

At the time the monument to Prince Hall was dedicated in the year 1895 by the colored Masons of the United States, J. J. Smith, Past Grand Master, conducted the ceremonies. He was made a Mason in African Lodge in 1846, and there were yet living a large number of Masons who had received their degrees in this Lodge.

Another unfounded story was circulated, unsupported by any evidence, that African Lodge No. 459 had changed its name to Celestial Lodge at some time about 1846. The Grand Secretary of Prince Hall Grand Lodge of Massachusetts denied that such a change was made, and stated, "African Lodge No. 459 simply changed its name to Prince Hall Grand Lodge after the passing of Prince Hall, for no other reason than to bear the name of the Father of Masonry among our people. It has ever since been known as the M.W. Prince Hall Grand Lodge, Free and Accepted Masons, of the State of Massachusetts, under which name it is incorporated."

This gives plausible explanations of the origin of the charges that African Lodge No. 459 became dormant, surrendered its charter, etc. It is an example of a case where a senior private Lodge developed into a Grand Lodge, as explained in following pages. Such cases, while not often encountered, are not unknown in Masonic history.

It has been suggested by Gould that the Grand Committee of the "Ancients", which developed into a Grand Lodge was originally their senior private Lodge; the Grand Chapter of the "Moderns" had its origin in a private chapter, and for a time St. Andrew's Lodge was the only constituent of St. Andrew's Provincial Grand Lodge. It is not too much to suppose that a situation of this kind was the case with both African Lodge of Boston and African Lodge of Philadelphia, both losing their original identity when the Grand organizations were established.

Very little evidence exists to indicate that contemporary Masons of Boston doubted or challenged

the legality or legitimacy of African Lodge No. 459.
Hall indicated at no time in his voluminous correspondence that the Lodge had been the subject of
attack on these or any other grounds. Should such
charges have been made, or any objections advanced,
Hall would probably have invoked the aid of England
in defense. It would appear to be a later generation
of Masons which made such an effort to discredit
African Lodge by these unfounded and malicious
charges, and only for the purpose of tainting the
legitimacy of the Prince Hall and other Negro Masonic organizations. It is seen that, almost from its
inception in the United States, segregation and discrimination have been practiced against Negro Freemasonry, based upon spurious charges and allegations
which have no factual foundation, but which are
designed to keep Negro Masons from gaining the
recognition and position in the Masonic community
to which their genuine and real Masonic status en-
titles them.

CHAPTER III

THE GRAND LODGE

Grand Lodges, as we know them today, gradually developed over a long period of years before becoming the highly organized and efficiently functioning bodies that they are today.

The Grand Lodge system originated in England in 1717, when members of four London and Westminster Lodges met in assembly and projected the first Grand Lodge. Prior to that time, the Grand Masonic Assembly, which was little more than a loosely organized meeting of Masons was the nearest thing to a Grand Lodge, although little is known of the proceedings or character of such assemblies, as very few records extant shed any light on their activities and organization. They do not appear to have had any Lodge creating powers, or to have held any actual authority over the Lodges, as each Lodge was sovereign in its own right and responsible to no higher authority.

Lodges of those times were often organized without any permit, license, dispensation or warrant whatever. When a number of Masons located in the same place met, they formed a Lodge, and when they dispersed, dissolved the Lodge with as little formality. Some such Lodges became permanent institutions and exist at this time. An example of such a self-constituted Lodge is that of a group from the Lodge of Edinburgh (Mary's Chapel), which seceded and formed the Lodge Cannongate and Leith, now No. 5 on the register of Scottish Lodges. Another is that of Journeyman Lodge No. 8. Both of these Lodges were self-constituted in defiance of the parent body.

The meeting of 1717 attempted to reduce this confusion and establish more stability and regularity in the formation of new Lodges. It made the Grand Lodge a delegate body, and established new regulations requiring a permit to be issued by the Grand Master before permitting Masons to assemble and work as a Lodge under authority of the Grand Lodge. The Grand Lodge thus acquired an ascendancy over constituent or private Lodges, although not without a certain amount of opposition from such "subordinate" Lodges. Certain of these continued to meet and conduct their Lodges in accordance with what was considered immemorial custom and usage and in particular objected to the new Grand Lodge regulation which required the authority of the Grand Master to constitute their Lodges. It was felt by a considerable number of these "private" Lodges that the new Grand Lodge was encroaching upon and restricting their ancient customs and activities, and they withheld conformation and allegiance from it for that reason.

This particular regulation was misinterpreted by many as an innovation in defiance of the old land-

marks. The reason for its adoption, however, was an
obvious one: to bring some semblance of formal order
and organization to the administration of the Masonic
structure. It merely required that proper Masonic
authority sanction the organization of its own subordinates, thus clearly restricting and controlling
indiscriminate or undesirable organization. The rule
originally applied only to London and Westminster.

During the Colonial period Grand Lodges were
formed by various other methods. The Ancients and
Moderns in England formed Grand Lodges under
ancient custom and usage. A private Lodge, by
assuming the powers and functions of a Grand Lodge
would thus organize and become a Grand Lodge.
There appears to have been no exact criteria or
pattern; when a Lodge became strong enough it
could become a Grand Lodge and constitute subordinate Lodges. After the assembly of 1717 it became
accepted practice that three or more Lodges could
take appropriate action, form a new Grand Lodge,
and work under new charters from the Grand body
which they had themselves created.

Grand Masters could appoint deputies or Provincial Grand Masters to act for them in constituting
and governing Lodges outside the seat of their authority. The Grand Master either possessed this power
or assumed it, and could act without reference to his
Grand Lodge. There were numbers of such appoint-

ments or deputations of the Grand Master's powers which do not appear in early records. Most of the early Lodges in America were founded by or through the operation of these deputies, or Provincial Grand Masters, as they were titled. Of these American appointments, the authenticity of many is beyond question, although there is some doubt as to the regularity of others. However, they are not challenged today, nor were they during the past, the regularity and legality of their work being accepted without question.

Since the Provincial Grand Master was appointed primarily for the constitution of Masons in his jurisdiction into Lodges, and to ensure that they were enrolled in the Grand Register, neither he nor his office constituted a Grand Lodge. He did not possess sovereign power, permanence or independence, and was appointed to function only as an administrative convenience.

It has been asserted that Prince Hall was commissioned as a Provincial Grand Master, even though English records do not record such an appointment. A review of the organization of African Grand Lodge will indicate the basis on which such an assumption is based, as well as to provide a clearer picture of the state of Masonry then existing in Boston and its relation to Negro Freemasonry.

On June 24, 1791, on the call of Prince Hall, a general assembly of the Craft was held at Boston, and African Grand Lodge was organized. Prince Hall was elected as Grand Master, Nero Prince as Deputy Grand Master, and a complete roster of elected and appointive officials was installed. All this was done in accordance with ancient custom and usage, and according to the methods in vogue and accepted at that time. White Masons of Boston, members of St. Andrew's Lodge, assisted in the installation ceremonies for the new Grand Officers. African Grand Lodge was thus constituted in effect as a provincial grand body, on the same level with St. John's and St. Andrew's provincial organizations. Though it was organized by different methods, it possessed equally as much regularity and legality, a fact tacitly admitted by the participation of St. Andrew's Lodge in the installation ceremonies.

The undeniable fact that Hall thereafter functioned actively as a Grand Master, and that a full list of Grand Officers was selected at this assembly indicates strongly that this was the first Grand Lodge. This same meeting marked the formal transition of African Lodge No. 459 into a Grand Body, especially as to the power to create new Lodges, which was evidently the purpose of the meeting. The organization of African Grand Lodge was regular and legal in every respect and had substantial precedent in America. Grand Lodges had been formed in like manner in Pennsylvania, Massachusetts and New

Jersey. At the death of the Provincial Grand Master Warren the St. Andrew Provincial Grand Lodge called a meeting and elected Joseph Webb as Grand Master, as well as a full slate of other Grand Officers, thereby forming a Grand Lodge. This was later reorganized and became the Massachusetts Grand Lodge of Ancient Masons, by union with the present Grand Lodge of Massachusetts in 1792.

In December, 1787, an assembly of Masons formed the first Grand Lodge of New Jersey. They met as individuals and not as delegates, and erected their Grand Lodge in the same manner as that of African Grand Lodge. The Grand Lodge of New Jersey has not been challenged, and it is accepted as having been legally and properly constituted. As in the case of African Grand Lodge, all requirements of Masonic law in force at that time had been met. A further indication of this is that St. Andrew's Lodge and its successors were later merged into the present Grand Lodge of Massachusetts.

White Masons in Boston were fully aware of the Negro membership of African Lodge No. 459 and African Grand Lodge. No objection or protest appears to have been made. Had their origin been considered illegal, irregular or in any way improper, it is certain that their right to exist would have been challenged. Had the territory of any Grand Lodge been considered "invaded" a protest would most certainly have been placed on record immediately. African Grand Lodge was erected openly, and was visited frequently by white Masons. From these premises it appears that objections to African Grand Lodge were not made until a much later time, when the controversy over Negro Masonry was at its height.

The tradition that Prince Hall was deputized or commissioned a Provincial Grand Master by the Grand Master of England is held by many to be based on fact, although no conclusive evidence to prove or disprove such a supposition has been found. The absence of any such record showing the appointment is not in itself significant, as we know that English records of that time were not accurately maintained. Further, such deputations were issued by Grand Masters without reference to their Grand bodies, and many such deputations are known to have been issued which were not recorded. There is no mention of any such appointment or deputation in Prince Hall's letter-book, and while the issuance of such a document would probably have resulted in some correspondence, none has been found. No Masonic acts were performed by Hall referring to the authority of the alleged deputation, and when African Grand Lodge was organized in 1791 it is not referred to as authority for the assembly.

Grimshaw, however, prints a copy of what purports to be the original patent, allegedly dated January 27, 1791. No claim is made that the printing is from the original, but he states that it was taken from a copy left by Hall with the Lodges he established in Philadelphia, and which was later found in their records. The copy bears the signature of Rawdon, Acting Grand Master. The Acting Grand Master at that time was Lord Rawdon, Earl of Moira, a distinguished soldier who, at the age of twenty-one was an officer in the British Army stationed at Boston. It is possible that he knew Hall personally.

While leading Negro Masons themselves were skeptical of the authenticity of this document when it appeared in Grimshaw's History of Negro Freemasonry, the deputation was upheld as genuine by other writers, who justified their claims by several facts and the inferences to be drawn from them.

The style of address frequently used by the British Grand Secretary when in correspondence with Hall was "Right Worshipful", which salutation, it is asserted, was used only in addressing Grand Officers. While this is true today it was not true in the time of Prince Hall. A fee of one guinea was exacted for registering the name of each Provincial Grand Master, and a one guinea fee was sent to William White, Grand Secretary of the English Grand Lodge, which was acknowledged August 20, 1792. This follows the date of the alleged deputation closely, and might appear to be a Provincial's fee, but equally plausible evidence indicates that it was another donation to the Grand Charity, and it appears as such on the records of the Grand Charity Fund under date of April 18, 1792.

Even though the evidence that Prince Hall received such a patent or deputation is not conclusive, there is no reason to believe that he did not have some special authority, and much evidence to support the contention that he did have special powers.

At the time Prince Hall applied for the warrant for African Lodge No. 459, it was sent directly to him, and his Lodge was organized by him. He was not referred to John Rowe, Provincial Grand Master for Massachusetts, who operated under a deputation issued to him in 1768 by the Grand Lodge which granted Prince Hall his charter. Prince Hall, and not John Rowe, was charged to "take care that all brethren were legally made Masons" and it required Hall, not Rowe, to send a written account of his actions under the warrant. This obviously granted to Prince Hall an authority at least equal to that of John Rowe, who was Provincial Grand Master of the same Grand Lodge which originally charted Prince Hall and his group.

Peter Mantore applied to Prince Hall in 1797 for authority to open a Lodge in Philadelphia, and addressed his application to "The Right Worshipful Prince Hall of the African Grand Lodge No. 459 of

Boston". This appears to indicate that Hall was considered the properly appointed Masonic authority to whom the application should be made. Mantore continued: "We congratulate you for having been invested with this high and holy trust conferred upon you by the authorities in England, together with your success in obtaining the Warrant constituting African Lodge No. 459." From this it is clear that Mantore believed Hall to be deputized or appointed to some higher office than that of Master of African Lodge No. 459, and the direct reference to the warrant appears to preclude the possibility that he was speaking of it alone. The "high and holy trust" could only have been some other power or authority and Mantore's reference to it bears out the theory that Hall was believed to have such greater authority.

Hall's reply to Mantore said, "we are willing to set you at work under our charter," and, "we hereby and herein give you license to assemble and work as aforesaid". He adds, "I would not advise you to take in any at present till your officers and Master be in the Grand Lodge, when we are willing to when he thinks convenient, and he may receive a full warrant instead of a permit". Hall apparently had the authority to grant both the warrant and the permit, and it appears from this that Hall acted as a Grand Master.

Prince Hall's letter of June 15, 1802 to the English Grand Secretary refers to "an account of my

brethren of the African Lodge which the Grand
Lodge hath honored me to take charge, and have by
the blessing of God endeavored to fulfill my obligations and the great trust you have reposed in me".

The phrase "great trust you have reposed in me"
indicates something more than his authority as Master, such as an appointment or grant of superior
authority.

Hall promptly granted the application of Mantore, and the fact that Hall was willing to issue a
"full warrant" proves that a separate Lodge was to
be constituted. The warrant was later issued, and the
officers of the new Lodge installed by Prince Hall
and his Grand Wardens on September 22, 1797.

Mantore's Lodge seems to have been a temporary
organization, all of the members having received their
degrees abroad, and as a self-constituted Lodge under
ancient custom and usage, they desired that their
Lodge be regularized and made legitimate by the then
prevailing practice of working under warrants and
dispensations from a higher Masonic authority. Their
concern for the formalities of organization is shown
by the fact that they did not desire to "go to work"
until they had such a dispensation. The name of the
new Lodge, African Lodge of Pennsylvania, might
be interpreted as meaning that Hall had intended to
establish only a branch of African Lodge in Philadelphia, but it appears that the Philadelphia group

desired to establish an independent Lodge. The fact that Hall issued a full warrant supports the assumption that a separate Lodge was to be erected.

Minutes of the Philadelphia Lodge show that on Nov. 26, 1798, a resolution to change the name of the Lodge to Moses African Lodge or James Moses Lodge No. 1 was introduced. James Moses was a prominent member of the Lodge, and it is probably in his honor that this change was suggested. While the resolution seems to have been passed, it was vetoed by Prince Hall. This suggests another example of Prince Hall's use of the authority of a Grand Master.

The Philadelphia Lodge, as in the case of African Lodge No. 459, was openly founded, and no record of any complaints or protests by white Masons has been found. There was no complaint alleging invasion of jurisdiction nor any objection of which a record is available against the erection of this Negro Lodge.

Hiram Lodge No. 3 of Providence, Rhode Island, was the third of the Negro Lodges to be organized. It is known that there were among the members of African Lodge No. 459 Masons who were residents of Providence. In his St. John's Day sermon at Charleston on June 25, 1792, Hall refers to his "dear brethren from Providence, who are at a distance from and cannot attend the Lodge here but seldom", and he wished them a safe return. This indicated that the Providence brethren had been in attendance on pre-

vious occasions and that they had made the difficult
trip from Providence for the purpose of attending
the Lodge.

On June 25, 1797, Hiram Lodge No. 3 was warranted. The Lodge is believed to have had nine
charter members, but their names are not known, and,
as the first charter has disappeared, the names of the
first officers cannot be given. No application seems
to have been made, nor was there a dispensation recorded; the group from Providence simply being set
up as a separate Lodge. This action followed a precedent set by the Grand Lodge of Scotland, when in
1794 it permitted Journeyman Lodge No. 8 to "grant
dispensations to open a Lodge at any place where a
number of their brethren were stationed". Following
this precedent made it unnecessary to enter into the
usual preliminaries involved when a new Lodge was
to be formed. The principal purpose in creating the
Lodge seems to have been to avoid the difficulty of
attending Lodge in Boston and the Providence Lodge
seems to have been set up when there were a sufficient number of Masons in Providence to justify its
organization.

When, in 1808, the African Grand Lodge was reorganized in Boston, delegates from Hiram Lodge No.
3 attended and took part. The records do not show
the names of the officers or delegates.

After 1808 Hiram Lodge appears to have become
more or less inactive, or dormant. The reasons for

this are largely a matter of conjecture. It has been
suggested that some of its members emigrated to
Liberia after 1813 to settle there as part of one of the
colonization programs, and that their absence made
proper functioning of the Lodge difficult. In 1826,
however, interest in the Lodge was renewed and relations with the Grand Lodge in Boston revived. The
minutes of the Grand Lodge for the meeting of
August 21, 1826 indicate that a committee was appointed to travel to Providence and to examine the
Lodge there and "if found worthy to give them a
Charter or Warrant".

Authorization of a warrant would tend to show
that the original warrant issued by Prince Hall had
been lost, or possibly taken by the members who had
emigrated. The Grand Lodge's action gave an impetus
to Hiram Lodge No. 3, and as the examination was
productive of a favorable answer, a new warrant was
issued on December 11, 1826, under the name Harmony Lodge No. 1. The Grand Lodge on October 5,
1827 indicated in its minutes receipt of an invitation
from Harmony Lodge No. 1 to assist in the dedication of a new hall in Providence. The brethren of
Harmony Lodge attended St. John's Day services in
Boston on June 24, 1827.

In reviewing the history of African Grand Lodge
as presented here, we see that it was organized in
1791 by Prince Hall and his fraters in accordance with

ancient custom and usage. Lodges were warranted in 1797 in Philadelphia and in Providence by Prince Hall as Grand Master. In 1808 a convention of delegates from the three then existing Negro Lodges met and reorganized into the first Grand Lodge. All of these things were done in accordance with the accepted Masonic practices of those times, and the record is singularly free from irregularities. Many other Masonic organizations of that time do not have such a fine record.

The effect of informalities in organization, wherever they occurred, is the important point, and it must be admitted by both white and Negro Masons that except for the attacks on Negro Masonry inspired by prejudice or controversy, they had little or no effect.

On June 8, 1808 representatives of African Lodge No. 459, Hiram Lodge No. 3 and African Lodge of Pennsylvania met in convention at Boston. This meeting, called by Nero Prince, was for the purpose of honoring Prince Hall, who died on December 4, 1807, and electing a successor to his office as Grand Master. The meeting has been described by Grimshaw as an "assembly"; other writers have referred to it as the organization of the first Negro Grand Lodge. The latter version is the more accepted, as it was apparently a delegate body. Grimshaw says that a New York Lodge was represented, but according to his own tables, this was in error, as he gives 1812 as the date of the first New York Lodge. Upton considers the meeting as the origin of the first Grand Lodge, although he says there are "traces" of an earlier Grand organization. Among the evidence he cites is the license given to Negro Masons of Philadelphia by Hall, and the certificate given to John Dodd by Hall in 1792. This document has been preserved, and reads as follows:

Boston, February 16, 1792.
And the light shineth in darkness and the darkness comprehended not. Bro. John Dodd having requested a 'certificate', we - - - Recommend him, as we found him a true and lawful brother Mason, and his behaviour with us was orderly (and) decent. Dated at the Sign of the Golden Fleece in Water Street, Boston.

(Signed) Prince Hall, G. M.
Cyrus Forbes, S. G. W.
George Middleton, J. G. W."

This June 8, 1808 meeting resulted in the election of Nero Prince as Grand Master and changed the name of African Grand Lodge to Prince Hall Grand Lodge as a manner of indicating respect and honor to the deceased Grand Master. Prince, in addressing the meeting, announced that the Grand Lodge of England had sent letters expressing sorrow on the death of Prince Hall. Unfortunately, the letters have not been preserved, as they would probably have thrown considerable light on the standing of Hall in official Masonic company.

Prince Hall Grand Lodge continued the exercise of its supreme authority until 1815, when Pennsylvania formed its own Grand body and withdrew from its jurisdiction.

For a number of years after 1808 the Grand Lodge continued to be known as "Boston Grand Lodge", "African Grand Lodge", as well as "Prince Hall Grand Lodge". It is claimed by some writers that the name "Prince Hall Grand Lodge" was not used officially until after 1847, when a charter under that name was received from the National Grand Lodge. Officially, however, Prince Hall Grand Lodge gives the date of 1808 as the year of its founding, and in 1908 celebrated its centennial.

As the Grand Lodge was an unincorporated body, the necessity of using exact names and titles did not exist as it does today. The various names given above were used rather loosely after the change of name at the 1808 meeting. In 1847 the National Grand Lodge, then newly organized, issued charters to its constituent Lodges, and exact names and titles were then needed. The Prince Hall Grand Lodge was warranted under its correct name. Four Lodges in New York City, including Boyer Lodge, which was organized in 1812, and three others organized in 1826 all claimed Prince Hall Grand Lodge as their parent Grand Lodge, indicating that this name was in use as early as those dates, certainly before 1847.

On December 27, 1815, the three Lodges founded in Pennsylvania by the Prince Hall Grand Lodge of Massachusetts held an assembly of the Craft at Philadelphia and organized the First Independent African Grand Lodge of Philadelphia.

The next Lodge established by the Prince Hall Grand Lodge was the Boyer Lodge No. 1 at New York, sometimes known as the African Lodge of New York. After publication of certain Lodge notices in a local newspaper, it came to the attention of the Caucasian Grand Lodge of New York at a special session held October 7, 1818, being again discussed at sessions in 1819 and 1829. Boyer Lodge petitioned the Caucasian Grand Lodge for recognition in 1845, and at the 1846 session its petition was rejected, with a report to the effect that the Boyer Lodge must be regarded as a clandestine body. There is no evidence to indicate the basis on which this rejection was made, and it must be assumed in the absence of any other explanation that the only objection was to the color of the petitioners.

Meanwhile, many other Negro Lodges were erected at New York by the Massachusetts Grand Lodge, Celestial No. 2 at New York, Rising Sun No. 3

at Brooklyn, and Hiram No. 4 at New York. All were chartered in 1826. All were erected by the Prince Hall Grand Lodge of Massachusetts, although there is no complete agreement on this point. Some writers claim that Celestial Lodge No. 2 was established by Harmony Lodge of Pennsylvania, and Rising Sun No. 3 by the First Independent African Grand Lodge of Pennsylvania. Records indicate that a Lodge named Rising Sun existed in New York around 1840, but there is no conclusive proof that it had any connection with that established by Massachusetts.

New York's first Grand Body, Boyer Grand Lodge F&AM was erected March 18, 1845. It is said to have been named in honor of General Boyer, a Haitian soldier, and functioned until 1848 when a schism split the organization at the time of formation of the National Grand Lodge of North America, also known as the National Compact, in 1847. The four Lodges of the Boyer Grand Lodge refused to affiliate with the new National body, refusing to recognize any higher Masonic authority than that of their own State Grand Lodge, and they reorganized at a General Assembly in New York in October 1848, under the title of United Grand Lodge, Free and Accepted Masons.

With the death of the National Compact in 1877 Negro Freemasonry continued to develop, and its orderly and consistent growth has resulted in an im-

portant and healthy institution. While it is true that
there has been a certain amount of continuing friction
between Grand Lodges operating in the same states,
because of informalities and irregularities in constituting Lodges by unscrupulous persons after the demise of the National Compact, there is no reason to
believe that the faults in organization and various
departures from Masonic usage and practice cannot
be corrected and brought into line with proper
Masonic jurisprudence and usage. In certain states
forward looking Grand Masters have already taken
the lead in effecting such Masonic "cures" and
"healings", taking under their jurisdiction Lodges ir-
regularly formed, and, after proper investigation,
warranting them as subordinate Lodges. This course
cannot fail to have a beneficial effect on Negro
Masonry as a whole, and indicates the positive meas-
ures being taken by the most forward-looking of the
Negro Masonic leaders.

The Prince Hall sodality alone has Grand Lodges
in most states, with over four thousand seven hundred Lodges having more than three hundred and
eleven thousand members, and possessing over eleven
million dollars in assets. There is a Prince Hall Grand
Lodge in Canada and one in Liberia.

The attitude of many white Masons may be
exemplified by that of M. W. Bro. Denslow of Missouri, who writes, "the question of regularity or ir-

regularity of Prince Hall Grand Lodges is not one for discussion in these columns. The fact remains that they do exist, and are carrying on their labours in a manner satisfactory to themselves".

However, the question of regularity or irregularity has been resolved, for the Prince Hall Masons at least, by the Massachusetts Grand Lodge Report, which is printed in its entirety elsewhere in this work, and no longer admits any possible basis for attack on Prince Hall Masonry on those grounds. The evidence has been available all of the time, and while it has taken a long time for it to be examined, the action taken by Massachusetts is the first positive step that has been taken towards eventual acknowledgement that Negro Freemasonry as such is free from the faults upon which most of the attacks on it have been based. With this beginning and the changing social consciousness of the present day it is certain that eventually Negro Freemasonry will achieve the dignity and recognition that it should have.

CHAPTER IV

TERRITORIAL JURISDICTION

The doctrine of exclusive territorial jurisdiction, purely American in origin and not accepted by all Masonic scholars, has been used as the basis of many attacks on Negro Freemasonry, alleging its illegitimacy on the grounds that this doctrine had not been followed in the establishment of Negro Lodges. This doctrine provides that there can be but one Grand Lodge in each state, and that when such a State Grand Lodge is formed it and it alone becomes automatically the sole and supreme Masonic authority in that state, and also that all Lodges in that state must either give their allegiance to the Grand Lodge so formed or remain unrecognized.

The effect of this doctrine is to establish a monopoly or "trust" in Masonry, as it compels all Lodges and Masons, whether willing or not, to become subordinate and subservient to the Grand Lodge of that state.

Attacks on Negro Lodges, particularly the Prince Hall Grand Lodges, have been repeatedly made and explained by invoking this doctrine. This is patently absurd, as shown by the recorded cases of violation of this principle by white Lodges themselves, and far from reflecting on the legitimacy of the Prince Hall Lodges, rather indicts the Grand Lodge of England under whose warrant the first Lodge of Negro Free-masons was constituted.

In 1874, when the Grand Lodge of England is-sued its warrant to African Lodge No. 459, there existed in Boston not one but two Provincial Grand Lodges, one of Scottish and one of English origin. If the charge of "invasion of jurisdiction" is to be made at all, it must be made against the Grand Lodge of England and not against the Prince Hall Lodge, as obviously the Grand Lodge of England, in warrant-ing African Lodge No. 459 intruded into the territory of both of the Provincial Grand Lodges already es-tablished in Boston.

In 1876 The Grand Lodge of England warranted Lodge No. 236 at Charleston, South Carolina, and the Provincial Grand Lodge of Pennsylvania chartered three Lodges there, although a sovereign and inde-pendent Grand Lodge had already been established.

The Grand Lodge of Missouri erected Lodges in Illinois in the year 1840, even though an Illinois Grand Lodge was already in existence in that state; Massa-chusetts constituted Lodges in Chile even after Chile had formed its own Supreme Council, and West Vir-ginia Lodges were established by the Grand Lodge of Virginia under similar circumstances.

As many as four different Grand bodies existed at one time in England; the Grand Lodge of the "Moderns", the Grand Lodge of the "Ancients", the

Grand Lodge of All England at York, and the Grand Lodge of England South of the River Trent. All of these operated concurrently in the same territory even after Negro Masons formed their first Grand Lodge in the United States. The original warrant issued to African Lodge No. 459 shows that it was issued by "The Grand Master of the Most Ancient and Honorable Society of Free Masons", and the seal contains the inscription, "The Seal of the Grand Lodge of Masons—London".

It would thus appear that the legitimacy of many present-day white Lodges could be challenged on precisely the same grounds of "illegitimacy" and with equally as much reason. The loosely organized Masonic structure of the 18th and 19th centuries seems to have permitted considerably greater laxity and informality in the organization and constituting of Lodges than would be possible today, and the doctrine of territorial jurisdiction, of which so much has been made by enemies of Negro Freemasonry did not exist at the time African Lodge No. 459 was constituted. Its legitimacy cannot longer be questioned; in fact, it is acknowledged by most Masonic students and confirmed by the Massachusetts Grand Lodge in its quarterly report of March 12, 1947.

If it is held that the Prince Hall group, organized after the fashion of the time and according to the then prevailing proper Masonic usage is considered to be illegitimate and not to be recognized, then it must be held by the same process of reasoning that many white Lodges which are today operating and accepted without question must also be held clandestine and spurious. If the premise of territorial jurisdiction is to be considered retroactive, which would be stretching the imagination over far, not only the Prince Hall group but all of those previously mentioned and many others also must be declared clandestine and spurious as well, yet no suggestion has been advanced that the white Lodges named were in any way irregular. The criticisms and attacks inspired by the doctrine of territorial jurisdiction appear to have been reserved only for use against Negro Freemasonry, even though it is true enough that the original intention was to establish the sovereignty of the various State Grand Lodges and to bring the entire Masonic structure into a better semblance of formal order and organization.

To indicate a few more examples of the length to which various Grand Lodges themselves have resorted in violation of this doctrine, several more cases of dual, triple and multiple sovereignty are shown.

Lodges in Hawaii work under the Grand Lodge of California, but the Grand Lodge of Scotland also has Lodges there.

Subordinates of Grand Lodges of England, Ireland, Scotland and Holland exist today in South

Africa, and work in complete harmony without any question of jurisdictional rights arising.

A number of Lodges in North China are subordinate to the European and American Grand Lodges. Jurisdictional problems are non-existent, in fact, Grand Lodges of England, Ireland, Scotland, the Philippine Islands and Massachusetts have formed a Joint Advisory Council in that area. Massachusetts, by its participation and acceptance of this situation, thereby violates its own historic assertion of exclusive jurisdiction.

Lodges operate in Shanghai chartered by six different Grand Lodges. The Lux Orientis Lodge, under authority of the Grand Lodge of Vienna, was constituted on January 25, 1933, and Masons of many different nationalities shared in the consecration ceremonies.

An agreement entered into between the Grand Lodges of England and Holland in the year 1770 provided that neither Grand Lodge would erect new Lodges in territory under the control of the other. Even then, care was taken to ensure against coercing English Lodges in Holland into joining the Dutch Grand Lodge, and the treaty stipulated for their independent and unmolested existence. A like action, in 1898 was taken by the Grand Lodges of England and New Zealand. These agreements obviously provided only for future Lodges, and the treaties obviously reject the American doctrine of exclusive jurisdiction.

The point that emerges from this discussion of territorial jurisdiction is that whatever the original purpose or intent may have been, it has been used against the institution of Negro Freemasonry exclusively in an attempt to taint its legitimacy by casting doubts and slurs on its legal and proper origin. If the same charges were made against many of the white Lodges named, it would be equally as logical to support them by the same premises as used against the Negro Lodges.

Obviously the desiderata was not primarily to establish, except by indirection, the legality or legitimacy of the Negro Lodges origin, but to besmirch them in any manner possible because of prejudice against their color. The doctrine of exclusive territorial jurisdiction became merely a peg on which to hang an excuse for prejudice against Negro Masonry.

CHAPTER V

THE NATIONAL COMPACT GRAND LODGE

In the year 1847 an organization was formed in Boston which was to become the subject of considerable controversy from its inception until long after its dissolution in 1877. Even today it is frequently discussed and the Lodges chartered by it challenged as "spurious" and "clandestine". There is no question but what it had a very ill influence on the development of Negro Freemasonry, despite the well-meaning intentions of its founders.

This was the National Compact Grand Lodge of North America, and it was organized principally to resolve differences among Negro Lodges, and to bring the entire structure of Negro Freemasonry into harmony and agreement, but the final result of its turbulent career was to spread even more dissension among Negro Masons than the cause it was supposed to cure could ever have done.

The background of this organization throws considerable light on the questions of the regularity or legitimacy of certain Negro Lodges and Grand Lodges, and indicates how the charges of "clandestine" and "spurious" originally arose in connection with Lodges chartered by it.

In the year 1828 the charter of Harmony Lodge No. 5 of Philadelphia, which had been working under the First Independent African Grand Lodge of Pennsylvania was revoked. The First Independent African Grand Lodge of Pennsylvania was the second Negro Grand Lodge to be formed, and was organized regularly by Lodges originally chartered by the Prince Hall Grand Lodge of Massachusetts. These Pennsylvania Lodges formed their own Grand Lodge on December 27, 1815, and Harmony Lodge No. 5, being charged with contumacy, was erased from the register.

Five years later in 1833 the members of Harmony Lodge No. 5, together with Union Lodge No. 4, which had been removed from the register at the same time, petitioned for a new charter, making their petition through a lodge in Norristown. The Norristown Lodge is believed to have been working under the Grand Lodge of Ohio (Caucasian). Each of these two Lodges paid one-half of a One Hundred and Twenty-Five Dollar fee, and were chartered on May 7, 1833, under the original name of Harmony Lodge No. 5. Union Lodge No. 4 as well as other Lodges appear to have worked under this same charter by dispensations which seem to have been granted by Harmony Lodge No. 5.

In 1837 these same Lodges met in Philadelphia and proceeded to organize the Hiram Grand Lodge of Pennsylvania, which functioned for about ten years. The existence of both Hiram Grand Lodge and the First Independent African Grand Lodge in the same state caused considerable dissension among

Negro Masons in Pennsylvania for some time. Hiram Lodge became powerful, with a steadily growing membership, while the First Independent African Grand Lodge steadily lost ground and influence.

Organization of the Hiram Grand Lodge was challenged by the First Independent African Grand Lodge, which attacked the charter, denying that the Grand Lodge of Ohio had ever met in Chillicothe, where the original charter was supposed to have been signed. This denial was supported by a circular published in 1847 and signed by the Grand Master of the Grand Lodge of Ohio (white) in which the Grand Lodge denied that it had met in Chillicothe at the time the charter was supposed to have been signed, denied that Harmony Lodge No. 5 was on its register, and denied that it had ever had officers named as signatories on the charter. It also denied that it had any Lodges at all in Pennsylvania or in any other state where a Grand Lodge was already in existence. In short, both the First Independent African Grand Lodge of Pennsylvania and the Grand Lodge of Ohio (white) asserted that the charter was not genuine, that it had not been issued by the Grand Lodge of Ohio, and that the name of the place where it was supposed to have been granted was false, as were the names of the officers whose supposed signatures appeared on the document. The proponents of Hiram Grand Lodge continued to maintain that the charter was genuine and was granted in proper form at the

NEGRO FREEMASONRY AND SEGREGATION

time and place indicated, and signed by properly authorized officers of the Grand Lodge of Ohio. These claims and counter-claims had, as they could not fail to have, a very disturbing effect on the status of Negro Freemasonry in Pennsylvania.

This internecine quarreling and dissension grew worse as time went on, and gave no indication of lessening. Relations between the two factions grew steadily worse, and deteriorated so steadily that leading Negro Masons realized that action must be taken to prevent any more damage than was already done to the entire Masonic fraternity. John T. Hilton, Grand Master of the Prince Hall Grand Lodge of Massachusetts took the first step by issuing a convention call to delegates from the Boyer Grand Lodge of New York, his own Prince Hall Grand Lodge of Massachusetts, The Hiram Grand Lodge of Pennsylvania and the First Independent African Grand Lodge of Pennsylvania, to meet at Boston on June 23, 1847.

The proceedings of this group have never been adequately reported, although it is known that the deliberations, over a period of several days, were quite turbulent. The net result of the convention was that a new Grand Body was formed, which became known as the National Compact Grand Lodge of North America. It is said that this action was taken by the convention without the presence of some of the delegates, but the record is no clearer on this point. The action in forming a new supreme body was all the more astonishing in the absence of instructed delegate authority and the limitations of the convention call.

The National Compact Grand Lodge was intended to be of a purely advisory nature, meant to promote the growth and well-being of Negro Masonry, to provide uniformity in the ritual, to bring the various state Grand bodies into closer harmony, and to provide a means of settling jurisdictional and other disputes when voluntarily submitted to it by contending parties. Up to this point it followed the general outline of the planned National Grand Lodge of North America (white) which had attempted organization in Baltimore during 1843, but had failed through lack of support.

Within a short time after the founding of the National Compact, it claimed supreme authority among Negro Lodges, assumed the right to grant charters to State Grand Lodges, and introduced into the third degree an obligation to obey its edicts under penalty of being outlawed from the Masonic fraternity.

The assumption of such extraordinary powers as the National Compact arrogated to itself is without precedent in Masonic History. In direct violation of the landmarks in its seizure of the supreme authority which had always been, by custom and usage, the prerogative of the State Grand Lodges, it yet might have become, in slightly different form and without

NEGRO FREEMASONRY AND SEGREGATION

usurping the powers and privileges of the State Grand Lodges, an influential and benign force in Masonry. This, however, was precluded by the arrogance of its self-constituted authority and the manner in which it was used.

Such abuses as making Masons "at sight" were common, and had the effect of making Masonic affiliation a purchaseable commodity, so openly were degrees sold. "Special dispensations" were sold cheaply, and some unscrupulous Masons set up several Lodges in five or six states clandestinely and by using the name of former National Grand Masters, even after the final dissolution of the National Compact. The result was a number of clandestine Lodges whose continued existence was and is a continuous reproach to the Craft.

Several of the Grand bodies withdrew from the National Compact within a short time, and considerable dissatisfaction was voiced by its members with the policies and management of the Compact. Internal politics of the organization also contributed to the confusion, and hastened its demise in 1877.

The spurious charters and dispensations sold even after its end brought more ill-repute to the already dead organization and the men who had dishonestly organized them. The last National Grand Master, Richard W. Greaves, denounced those who attempted to continue under its "authority", fraudulently setting up Lodges under the spurious authority of a defunct organization. Most of the spurious Negro Freemasonry existing today, according to Davies, "traces its origin to this curious hybrid" (National Compact).

The eventual failure of the National Compact appears to have been foreseen by one of the groups whose delegates attended its founding. After the Boston meeting at which it was brought into being, the delegates from Boyer Grand Lodge returned to New York and reported the action they had taken to the Grand Lodge. The four Lodges of the Boyer Grand Lodge, however, repudiated the National Compact and refused to recognize its validity. At their General Assembly in New York on October 13, 1848, they underwent a reorganization, adopting the name of United Grand Lodge, Free and Accepted Masons. Their action was followed by Negro Masons in Philadelphia, all of which tended to increase the confusion and complexity of the problem already created by the formation of the National Compact.

It must be admitted that the founders of the National Compact appear to have been motivated by a commendable desire to stop the factional strife which was then disrupting Negro Masonry. Its failure was due to other considerations, but whatever the reasons for it, the harm done to Negro Freemasonry was and is incalculable.

CHAPTER VI

CONTROVERSIAL INCIDENTS IN THE GROWTH OF NEGRO MASONRY

Negro Freemasonry in the United States and the conditions under which it operates have not changed appreciably since the turn of the century, although the number of Negro Masons has increased steadily. It has been estimated by Voorhis that one of every eight Freemasons in this country is a Negro. Colored Grand Lodges now function in thirty-eight states, as well as in Canada and Liberia. Accurate statistics are not available, yet it may safely be presumed that there are well over one-half million Negro Freemasons today. With the rapidly changing social pattern of this country it is probable that with the growth of tolerance and the approaching end of segregation much greater progress will be made by the Negro Freemasons as well as the entire Negro race. Recognition of the rightful and legitimate standing of the Negro Freemason is nearer each year, and has been greatly advanced by the action of the Massachusetts Grand Lodge (Caucasian) whose report on Negro Freemasonry, published elsewhere in this work, has served to focus new attention on the important question of recognition.

Negro Lodges and Grand Lodges operate in much the same way as white Lodges, whose organizational structures and activities resemble them greatly. Since both derive from the Grand Lodge of England, the "work" is also similar, varying little from one Grand Jurisdiction to another, just as the "work" of the white Lodges varies. There is no fundamental difference between them in organization, and the rules under which they are established and governed. Negro Lodges as well as white have adopted the principle of Exclusive Territorial Jurisdiction and apply it in about the same manner.

Some Negro Grand Lodges have been recognized by foreign Grand Lodges, as well as by white Grand Lodges in the United States. The matter of recognition is one determined by the Grand Lodges themselves, as they alone determine the basis for recognition, and can grant or refuse such recognition as they see fit.

It appears difficult to understand how any Grand Lodge or subordinate body could justify its refusal to recognize Negro Freemasonry after a study of its history and origin, stemming from the admittedly highest Masonic authority of that time, the Grand Lodge of England, and more particularly so when such a study would reveal the "irregularities" in the history and jurisprudence of many "recognized" Caucasian Grand Lodges. Withholding such recognition on the grounds of "illegitimacy" could hardly be justified without placing the Lodges making such

NEGRO FREEMASONRY AND SEGREGATION

charges in the same position as those they accuse. The action of the Massachusetts Grand Lodge makes the position of those jurisdictions which consistently refuse such recognition untenable, and establishes a precedent for future guidance.

Any reasons for continuing to withhold recognition must then be due to other factors than the regularity or irregularity of the Negro Lodges because of their origin. The Negro Freemason is not recognized only because he is a Negro, and not for reasons having to do with the legality or otherwise of his fraternal associations.

This prejudice has been demonstrated and proved times without number by the writings and utterances of white Masonic scholars and writers. A few of these are given here, but are by no means the bulk of the attacks on Negro Freemasonry.

Gen. Albert Pike, the celebrated author of "Morals and Dogma" and one of the leading American Masonic scholars had this to say of Negro Freemasonry: "that it was as regular as any other, but I took my obligation to white men, not Negroes. When I have to accept Negroes as brethren or leave Masonry, I shall leave it".

Pike's words certainly indicate that he was an enemy of Negro Freemasonry, and yet he presented the Ill. Thornton Jackson, Commander of the Southern Jurisdiction, Prince Hall, with copies of the Scottish Rite Manuals he had prepared, as well as the Grand Constitutions of 1762, the Latin Grand Constitutions of 1786, and the Statutes of the Supreme Council, Southern Jurisdiction, as published by Robert McCoy. These works from the basis of the work and practice of the Prince Hall Ancient and Accepted Scottish Rite.

This inconsistency indicates that Pike believed in the separation of the races socially and fraternally, but did not oppose the practice of Freemasonry by Negroes as an independent body. His objections appear to have been to the absorption or affiliation of Negro Freemasons with the general body of the Masonic fraternity.

Other attacks on Negro Freemasonry were more vicious. Their basis seems to be the assumption that the Negro is inferior in every way to the white man, and does not nor cannot possess the qualities of either character or intelligence sufficiently to embrace properly Masonry and Masonic teachings. One such example, from the pen of Frederick Speed, Grand Secretary of Mississippi, appeared in The Southland, a periodical published in Vicksburg, April 24, 1909, as follows: "but Scipio Africanus is simply a brute, with no revenge or resentments, and no regard for the truth or purity of his women. Whiskey, cocaine and miscegenation are his bane, and until some remedy is found for these great evils, the poor fellow will continue to go down lower and lower in the social scale until finally the time will come when he and the white man must part company".

In the Proceedings of the Grand Lodge of Illinois, 1899, Appendix 1, we read: "We know that Masonry is not only close in fellowship, but it is perfect in morals and intricate in Science. And we know that the Negroes of the South are wholly incompetent to embrace it. They are ignorant, uneducated, immoral, untruthful, and intellectually they are more impotent than minority or dotage—both of which we exclude. It would be rare if any locality could furnish the requisite number of sufficient capacity to open a Lodge. Therefore, to have Lodges exclusively of Negroes would be dangerous to the high character of our Order. And to associate them in Lodges with white brethren would be impossible".

Many other attacks upon Negro Freemasonry have been published and given wide circulation. They have ranged from mild attempts to make the Negro Freemason appear a ridiculous figure, aping the customs and manners of the white Masons, to savage and venomous diatribes condemning Negroes utterly, and not merely as Freemasons. A few of these are published in the Appendix to this work, and are illustrative of the methods employed by foes of Negro Freemasonry.

It must not be assumed that all Caucasian Masons joined in these attacks; Negro Freemasonry and the right of the Negro Freemason to recognition were defended by many Caucasian Lodges and Grand Lodges long before the Massachusetts decision. In various cases Grand Masters of white Lodges have extended recognition to Negro Lodges and have even bestowed charters upon new Lodges. Certain white Lodges have accepted Negro members from time to time without causing any dissension. White members of colored Lodges are known to have been initiated, and in one case at least a white Grand Lodge warranted an affiliated Lodge of both white and colored members.

This Lodge, Alpha Lodge No. 116, of Newark, New Jersey, was the subject of considerable factional and jurisdictional dispute for many years, and caused one of the most widely known incidents in the history of Negro Freemasonry, although until very recently most of the reports relating to it have been garbled and misinterpreted. After collating and studying all available original source material on the subject, Voorhis has furnished us the most widely accepted and probably the most historically accurate history of the whole controversy.

On January 27, 1791, Alpha Lodge No. 116, of Newark, New Jersey, was constituted under a charter from the Grand Lodge of New Jersey. Four days later, on January 31, it held its first regular Communication. Thirteen petitions for initiation were presented, one from John M. Hoon, a schoolteacher who was the only white man among the petitioners, and twelve Negroes. The petitions were referred to the investigating committee. Visitors were present at this meeting, and were thus aware of the identity of the twelve Negro petitioners, whose names had appeared on the petition to the Grand Lodge the previous year, when formation of the "Cushite" Lodge had been attempted and which petition was rejected.

The fact that twelve Negroes had petitioned Alpha Lodge soon became known, and was publicized by articles in the New York Sun and The Landmark, a Masonic publication. This news resulted in a petition being presented to the Grand Master, signed by over two hundred brethren, and dated February 24, 1871, which stated the belief of the petitioners that Alpha Lodge No. 116 had obtained its charter by deceit, and requested the Grand Master to take action to prevent the initiation of Negroes if they should be elected.

On February 28, 1871, the meeting was held, and after routine business, voted to elect John M. Hoon. A report was made by the Committee on the twelve colored men, and the Lodge prepared to ballot on their election.

At this juncture the Right Worshipful Brother Edwards, Grand Marshal, arrived, and was seated in the East with Grand honors. Invited to speak, he addressed the Worshipful Master and advised him that he carried a communication from the Grand Master. He then read the petition to the Grand Master which desired the Grand Master to stop the initiation of Negroes into the Lodge, and followed this by reading the letter from the Grand Master to the Lodge, which was practically an order to surrender the charter to Brother Edwards. In compliance with this order, the charter was handed to the Grand Marshal, who then closed the Lodge.

The arrest of the charter naturally caused considerable confusion, and it was not until almost a year later, in 1872, that the warrant was restored to Alpha Lodge, and then by a majority of one vote of the Grand Council. During the period the charter was under arrest the entire matter was investigated by the Committee, and on January 16, 1872 it was finally restored.

The restoration of the charter in 1872 was not, however, the end of the matter. Later in the same year, after Alpha Lodge No. 116 had admitted colored members, Trenton Lodge No. 5 passed resolutions against the initiation of colored men into the Fraternity, as tending to disturb the harmony of the Craft and as being of no benefit to them. Forwarded to every Lodge in the Jurisdiction, the resolutions requested appropriate action to stop such initiations.

Formal charges against Alpha Lodge No. 166 and its officers were filed on May 27, 1872; were read at

NEGRO FREEMASONRY AND SEGREGATION

the 1873 Communication and passed to the Committee on Jurisprudence. When filed, the Committee's report stated that the activities and conduct of Alpha Lodge No. 116 since its charter had been restored were in accordance with Masonic Law. The report was adopted by the Grand Lodge, and the complaining resolutions of Trenton Lodge No. 5 were declared out of order. This decision could hardly be disputed, as each Lodge is the sole judge of its applicants qualifications. It might be added that in the entire history of Alpha Lodge not one member has been expelled for un-Masonic conduct, which indicates that the Lodge selected for admission only candidates of high moral worth and integrity. Indeed, its first colored initiates included two ministers, teachers and professional men.

Thornburgh implies that the few white men who originally belonged to Alpha Lodge No. 116 gradually dropped out, and as only Negroes joined it, it became to all intents and purposes a Negro Lodge.

For over thirty years no important issues were raised relative to Alpha Lodge, although considerable discussion and difference of opinion had arisen between Grand Lodges on the matter. In his 1872 Annual Address the Grand Master of the Grand Lodge of Delaware recommended that Delaware Lodges be instructed not to have any Masonic intercourse with Alpha Lodge No. 116 of New Jersey. This was ap-

proved by the Grand Lodge, and such instructions
were issued to Delaware Lodges. The action of the
Grand Master was criticized by other Grand jurisdictions, as, although some of these did not approve
of Negro Freemasonry, they felt that jurisdictional
rights were involved which might establish a precedent affecting themselves.

The Mississippi Grand Master, who had been in
communication with the Grand Master of New Jersey
on the subject, recommended that the Mississippi
Committee on Foreign Correspondence sever fraternal
relations with New Jersey, but the Grand Lodge of
Mississippi, after considerable discussion, finally
adopted the following resolution: "That the Most
Worshipful Grand Lodge of Masons in New Jersey
has been found adequate to deal with the question
of admitting Negroes into membership with its subordinate Lodges, and it is the confident expectation
of this Grand Lodge that she also will be found adequate to meet the emergency presented by the action
of Alpha Lodge No. 116 of Newark, New Jersey".

In August, 1908, Edwin J. Martin, Grand Master
of Mississippi, wrote to William D. Wolfskeil, Grand
Master of New Jersey, stating that he had "heard
that there is a Lodge in your Grand Jurisdiction composed of Negroes, and that your Grand Lodge permits
the initiation and affiliation of Negroes as Masons".
He requested to be informed if this was true.

NEGRO FREEMASONRY AND SEGREGATION

The New Jersey Grand Master replied with a brief relation of the facts regarding Alpha Lodge No. 116. Several months later the Grand Master of Mississippi wrote again, saying, "Yours of August 25th, advising me that Negroes are initiated and affiliated in your Grand Jurisdiction is received. Our Grand Lodge holds differently. Masonry never contemplated that her privileges should be extended to a race totally morally and intellectually incapacitated to discharge the obligations which they assume or have conferred upon them in a Masonic Lodge. It is no answer that there are exceptions to this general character of the race. We legislate for the race and not for the exceptions. We hold that affiliation with Negroes is contrary to the teachings of Masonry, and is dangerous to the interest of the Fraternity of Free and Accepted Masons. Therefore I, E. J. Martin, Grand Master of Masons in the State of Mississippi, do order that fraternal correspondence between the Grand Lodge of Mississippi and the Most Worshipful Grand Lodge of New Jersey be and is hereby discontinued until such time as the Most Worshipful Grand Lodge of New Jersey shall see fit to desist from her present practice of initiating and affiliating Negroes as Masons. With my best personal regards, I am, sincerely yours, (signed) Edward J. Martin, Grand Master".

Grand Master Martin reported his actions to the Mississippi Grand Lodge in 1909 at the Annual Com-

74

munication, and a Special Committee of five was appointed to study the matter. At the 1910 Annual Communication, the Committee reported the results of their study to the Grand Lodge, which supported the action of Grand Master Martin.

In the 1927 Proceedings of the Grand Lodge of Mississippi the following paragraph appears, excerpted from an address by the M. W. John R. Tally: "Whereas, from a careful reading of the correspondence between the Grand Master of New Jersey and our Past Grand Master Ed Martin at the time fraternal relations were severed between this Grand Jurisdiction and New Jersey, I am convinced that the true situation was not understood by either of the Grand Masters. And, whereas, all other states that severed relations with New Jersey at the same time have long ago resumed their fraternal relations with that sister jurisdiction, Therefore, I think that the time has arrived when we should forget this difference and resume fraternal relations with the Grand Jurisdiction of New Jersey".

This had as its result the healing of the breach between the two jurisdictions, and in 1928, when it had been arranged to resume relations with New Jersey, Grand Master Howard R. Cruse, Grand Master of New Jersey, who was present, addressed the Grand Lodge of Mississippi and was cordially received.

The "Mississippi incident", as it was called, was completely closed when, on April 17, 1929, M. W.

NEGRO FREEMASONRY AND SEGREGATION

George D. Riley, Past Grand Master of Mississippi, returned the visit and was received with honor by the Grand Lodge of New Jersey.

After some discussion in other jurisdictions, the subject was finally dropped, although Oklahoma was the last to restore fraternal relations with New Jersey, which it did in 1914. In 1940 Oklahoma again severed relations with New Jersey, but restored them once more two years later.

In a brief summary of the history of Alpha Lodge No. 116, Grand Master Wolfskeil wrote, some time after its charter had been returned, "Of the conduct and administration of the affairs of Alpha Lodge, after its warrant had been returned to it, no one now alive may justly offer criticism. It may be safely assumed that every Grand Master succeeding William E. Pine kept that Lodge under watchful supervision, and became satisfied that every petitioner for membership was dealt with in literal and exact conformity to the rules of this Grand Lodge and the regulations governing the Craft".

From time to time Negroes have been admitted to membership in white Lodges, but such cases constitute exceptions to the general rule rather than indicate a general practice. Voorhis relates several such cases, and there are said to have been many more the details of which are not generally known. In all such cases of record that have been studied, the

Masonic conduct of the Negroes who were made Masons by white Lodges provided no cause for attack or complaint, indicating that the Negro Masons justified their membership by properly and faithfully discharging the duties entailed by their obligations.

There are also many examples of white Masons being initiated into Negro Lodges. Voorhis lists several of these, but does not include such prominent men as Marshall Field, the famous Chicago merchant and philanthropist, who became a member of North Star Lodge No. 1 (Prince Hall) of Chicago, or L. Fish, another prominent Chicago business leader who was initiated into the same Lodge.

Outside the continental limits of the United States Negroes have been accepted without question in many Lodges. Visitation by colored brethern to white Lodges has been welcomed, nor does the propriety of such fraternization appear to have been disputed. When the Grand Master of Liberia visited England in 1893, he was welcomed with honor by the Grand Lodge of England. The Scotch Grand Secretary, D. M. Lyon, and the Canadian editor of "The Craftsman" were made honorary members of the Grand Lodge of Liberia, all without any protest or untoward incidents recorded.

The attitude of European Masons towards recognition of colored brethern is entirely different from that prevailing in the United States. The social regime of European countries does not have the myriad problems that have complicated the question of race relationships here. Racial prejudices, which form the principal barrier to a full and complete recognition and acceptance of Negro Freemasonry in this country have their origin in conditions which have not existed in countries abroad. European Masons, for example, find it hard to understand how the Grand Lodge of New York can extend fraternal recognition to the Grand Lodge of Haiti, as they did in 1921, while refusing that same recognition to Negro Masons at home. At the time this occurred the Grand Lodge of Haiti was in fraternal relationship with many colored Grand Lodges in America, none of them recognized by New York.

There are numerous such curious and inconsistent episodes in the history of the Craft. The Grand Master of California refused to allow a white Mason the right to visit one of his Lodges, on the ground that the applicant would be violating the regulations of his own Grand Lodge, and that white Masons did not reciprocate. Equally inconsistent is the case of a colored Mason named Peter S. Henry, who was a member of Union Lodge at New Bedford, Massachusetts. He later joined the white Mount Hope Lodge at Fall River, Massachusetts, and when the New Bedford Lodge learned of this was tried and expelled. These two isolated cases show the same intolerance of which Negro Masons complain, and made them appear ridiculous.

On certain occasions white Masons, without extending formal recognition, have come to the assistance of Negro brethern. A case in point is that of Mt. Moriah Lodge No. 1 of Louisville, Kentucky, which was warranted by the Grand Lodge of Ohio, (Prince Hall) in 1850. The Lodge was prevented from holding its meetings in Louisville by the "black laws", and met in New Albany, Indiana, until 1853. During that year they attempted to hold a meeting in Louisville, and during the course of the meeting, the Lodge was raided and twenty-one members arrested. They were taken to the city jail, where the jailor refused to permit them to enter, and were freed on their own recognizance until the Court convened the next day. When they arrived at Court at the time set, they were not permitted to even enter the Court room, but were told to leave quietly and forget the matter. Needless to say, they did so, and no attempts were made to prevent their subsequent meetings. The explanation appears to lie in the fact that, according to Booker T. Washington, both the jailer and the judge were Masons, and came to the aid of their brethern in distress.

The origin of St. John's Lodge No. 50 (Prince Hall) of Sewickly, Pennsylvania, is not only interesting but unique. A white lodge of the same name and

NEGRO FREEMASONRY AND SEGREGATION

number was composed of prominent business and social figures, and had been in existence for many years. In the year 1890 the Lodge was alarmed by four Negro Masons, who desired admission. Judge J. W. White, then Master of the Lodge, saw no reason for withholding the privileges of Masonry from Masons, whatever their race or other status, and after the applicants were tried and proven, they were admitted to fellowship.

Upon learning of this, the Grand Lodge ruled that an apology from the Master was in order, with a promise not to repeat the "offense". The Master, Judge White, who was a highly respected jurist, saw no reason why such an apology should be forth-coming, and refused. The Grand Lodge then or-dered St. John's Lodge to prefer charges against its Master, but the members refused to do this. The Grand Lodge then suspended St. John's Lodge for ninety-nine years. Upon its dissolution, the ques-tion arose of what disposition to make of the Lodge room, with its beautiful furniture and appointments. This, however, seems to have solved itself in a most fitting manner.

On June 24, 1891, in a hall opposite St. John's Lodge rooms, twenty-six Negroes were initiated by the Grand Lodge of Pennsylvania (Prince Hall). On the night their officers were installed, they took over the entire Lodge room of St. John's Lodge No. 50, and were given a warrant under the same name and number as the suspended Lodge.

A colored Lodge in Panama, chartered in 1908 by the Grand Lodge of Scotland, and known as Thistle Lodge No. 1013, was the subject of some controversy. The Grand Lodge of Florida (Caucasian) claimed jurisdiction, according to their published proceedings for 1908. Their claims were ignored by the Grand Lodge of Scotland, and later the jurisdiction of the Canal Zone was taken over by Massachusetts. The doctrine of exclusive territorial jurisdiction, of which so much had been made, does not seem to have deterred either Florida or Massachusetts, or to have prevented them from attempting to seize powers and jurisdiction from the Grand Lodge of Scotland.

Three white Masons in Illinois in the year 1912 acted as pall bearers at the funeral of a Negro Mason. The Lodge to which they belonged was ordered to prefer charges against them, which resulted in the expulsion of one and the suspension of the other two members.

No useful purpose can be served by a detailed examination of all such cases on record—enough has been presented to indicate that the segregation of Negro Freemasons and discrimination against them was not practiced by all white Masonic bodies or individual Masons—and that, even at a time when it

NEGRO FREEMASONRY AND SEGREGATION

was unpopular to do so, Masons of each race made efforts to end the disgraceful practices which brought no credit to Masonry.

That their efforts were not more successful is perhaps due to the social climate of the time, which was not prepared for the principle of integration, but they have at least proved that Negro and white Masons can work together in perfect harmony and understanding once the artificial barriers are lifted.

While the cases presented in this chapter are by no means all on the credit side, it is apparent that the basis of most of the controversies studied is artificial, narrow and prejudiced. These factors should no longer prevent the closer understanding and rapprochement necessary for the proper and logical development of a better climate among Masons.

CHAPTER VII

NEGRO FREEMASONRY TODAY AND TOMORROW

The growth and development of Negro Free-masonry since the organization of Prince Hall Grand Lodge has been marked by a number of struggles and controversies, many of which have been briefly described in this work. Not the least of these difficulties has been the prejudiced attitude of many white Masons and Masonic bodies, who have steadily refused to recognize the historically accurate evidence which proves conclusively the legitimacy and regularity of the larger majority of Negro Lodges. While it is true that a certain number of cases leave some reason for doubt as to the regularity of their organization, the arguments used against them might well be applied to a number of Lodges composed exclusively of white Masons as well.

Negro Freemasonry in America stems from the organization of African Lodge No. 1, founded by Prince Hall, and the regularity and legality of its charter, granted by the authority of the Grand Master of the Grand Lodge of England, cannot be impugned, as the Prince Hall Grand Lodge, organized according to ancient custom and usage, has as its authority a charter issued by the highest authority of Masonry at that time in the entire world.

NEGRO FREEMASONRY AND SEGREGATION

Despite the discrimination and prejudice against Negro Freemasonry, the progress made in its long and bitter fight for recognition has been noteworthy, and in the immediate past few years has been very encouraging, even though much hard work must patiently be accomplished before prejudice and discrimination disappear altogether.

The labels "spurious" and "clandestine", so often used in attacks on all Negro Masonic organizations can no longer be used to apply to all Negro Lodges; the Massachusetts decision removes the taint of "illegitimacy" from the Prince Hall sodality and paves the way for a broader and more liberal acceptance of Negro Freemasonry generally as a legitimate and lawful institution, equally as much so as the Massachusetts Grand Lodge itself.

Recognition of other Negro Masonic bodies should be advanced by this decision as well. The "irregularities" and "informalities" of organization of which they are accused have their counterpart in the institutions of white Masonry, and, if the will to do so is present, can be "healed" in much the same ways. Precedents for such action may be found in the history of white Freemasonry, and may well be used to remove any such objections, if such actions are taken and received in good faith.

Such recognition will not come automatically. A tremendous amount of effort and cooperation on the part of all Negro Masonic bodies will be required. Before the main body of the Craft, excluding Prince Hall Freemasonry, which is already recognized as legitimate, can achieve the status of recognition, it must organize into a more closely knit entity and must present a united front. The various Negro Masonic bodies must show some sort of cohesion and unity if they wish to facilitate recognition by white Grand Lodges.

This will require more than cooperation—it means in addition to hard work that unanimity of purpose must be adopted—that compromises must be made—that in some cases jurisdictional rights may be effected, and that a single Supreme governing body may have to be established. Only by effecting harmony in its own ranks can Negro Freemasonry dignify itself sufficiently to warrant complete fraternal recognition.

In recognizing the legitimacy and regularity of the Prince Hall Masons, which an unbiased and impartial review of the evidence shows to be proper, the Massachusetts decision appears carefully to avoid the question of fraternization, except to say:

"The Committee believes that in view of the existing social conditions in our country, it is advisable for the official and organized activities of white and colored Freemasons to proceed in parallel lines, but organically separate and without mutually embarrassing demands or commitments."

This paragraph appears to sum up the general feeling among white Masons, and supplies the key to the whole situation in the words "existing social conditions". The question of the legitimacy or spurious origin and existence of Negro Freemasonry thus becomes merely an excuse upon which to base the implication that Negro Masons are somehow an inferior group and as such are not entitled to equality. This refrain is far from new, and has been used over and over again by those who withheld recognition of Negro Freemasonry with the excuse that it is a "spurious" or "clandestine" affair. Most of these men were either unwilling to admit or unaware of the fact established by the Massachusetts decision that Prince Hall Masonry was legitimate and lawfully constituted from its inception, something that not all white Lodges would dare to claim. These excuses and charges would disappear if all of Negro Freemasonry were to re-organize and regularize its Masonic status by the act of re-establishing its Lodges and Grand Lodges according to the recognized principles of Masonic jurisprudence.

It is ironic that Masonry, which has always been recognized as a force for morality and progress should or could be used for the purpose of suppressing any one group, particularly when these very qualities are those which could assist most greatly in removing the artificial barriers which separate the two races. The sense of degradation that attached itself to anything labelled, whether justly or not, inferior, must be removed. Certainly any tag or label which tends to degrade cannot have the effect of inspiring respect or tolerance, and the opposition of many to the institution of Negro Freemasonry may have been largely caused by such scorn, ridicule and belittling of an institution of which they may well have no personal knowledge.

The opportunities for leadership of the American Negroes have never been as great as they are today. While the integration of the colored race into our highly complex and involved social system cannot be accomplished in a short time, tremendous progress has already been made. Even in the South, where resistance to this change has been greatest, integration continues to show gains. The institutions of higher learning, which had previously discouraged, if not forbidden utterly the enrollment of Negroes, are now accepting more colored students than ever before. Negroes are entering the learned professions in large numbers, and while the impact on the social body of America has been felt, the prejudices accumulated over a long period of years are beginning, however slowly, to give way. With more and better educational facilities open to Negroes, and with more opportunities in business and the professions open to them, they are developing rapidly in every way. And as each year passes, Negroes are more and more taking an active part in government.

This continuing development offers a challenge to Freemasonry. With proper encouragement and cooperation, white Masonry could offer untold assistance to the leaders of the American Negroes. Negro Freemasonry offers no challenge to white Freemasons. There is no reason why such teamwork could not aid materially in the struggle of the Negroes to improve their position. As to the facts of integration, no realist can deny that it will soon be accomplished, and there is no reason save prejudice why the Negro Freemason cannot be recognized and helped. Surely it is not because of any fear of social fraternization, as except in rare instances in the past the Negro Freemasons have shown no indication of such presumption, and it appears at this crucial time in our history that social intercourse between the two races is only what individuals are willing to make it. In time all prejudice will disappear, but it will take considerable effort and intelligent understanding before all traces of such prejudices, which have been years in developing, completely vanish.

Freemasonry can play a very important part in shaping the future development of the Negro race.

NEGRO FREEMASONRY AND SEGREGATION

The Grand Masters of Negro Grand Lodges, as well as Negro Freemasons generally represent their highest type of men, and by friendly cooperation and assistance can, with the help of white Masonic leaders, make this traditional period considerably less difficult for both Negroes and whites.

Such harmony would create a climate of tolerant understanding and helpful assistance which could not fail to develop into a mutual respect and better fraternal relationship than at any time in the past.

In the appendix to this work will be found excerpts from the writings of various Masonic authors, together with material taken from the writings of figures prominent in public life. These are included for the purpose of illustrating how Negro Freemasonry has been presented to the reading public by a variety of writers. No comment is added—indeed, no comment is necessary. The reader will make his own points from what he reads, and thus will be made more acutely aware of the nature and form assumed by most attacks on Negro Freemasonry.

H.R.H. The Duke of Cumberland, Grand Master of the Grand
Lodge of England, who Chartered the First Negro Lodge in
America with Prince Hall as Grand Master.

APPENDIX

FIRST OFFICERS OF AFRICAN GRAND LODGE OF NORTH AMERICA

Prince Hall, Grand Master
Nero Prince, Deputy Grand Master
Cyrus Forbs, Senior Grand Warden
George Middleton, Junior Grand Warden
Peter Best, Grand Treasurer
Prince Taylor, Grand Secretary

AMERICAN NEGRO MASONS INITIATED INTO ARMY LODGE NO. 441 ON MARCH 6, 1775, AT BOSTON.

Prince Hall
Peter Best
Cuff Bufform
John Carter
Peter Freeman
Fortune Howard
Cyrus Jonbus
Prince Rees
Thomas Sanderson
Buesten Singer
Boston Smith
Cato Speain
Prince Taylor
Benjamin Tiber
Richard Tilley

TEXT OF ORIGINAL CHARTER ISSUED TO PRINCE HALL BY THE GRAND LODGE OF ENGLAND

Granted by the Grand Lodge of England ("Moderns") in the year 1784.

"Our Right Worshipful and Loving Brethren:

"We, Thomas Howard, under authority of His Royal Highness, Frederick, Duke of Cumberland, Grand Master of the Most Ancient and Honorable Society of Free and Accepted Ancient Masons sends Greeting:

"Know ye, that we at the humble petition of our Right Trusty and well beloved brethren, Prince Hall, Boston Smith, Thomas Saunderson, and several other brethren residing in Boston, New England, in North America, do hereby constitute the said brethren into a regular Lodge of Free and Accepted Masons, under the title or denomination of the African Lodge, to be opened in Boston aforesaid, and do further at their said petition and of the great trust and confidence reposed in every one of the above named brethren, hereby appoint the said Prince Hall to be Master, Boston Smith, Senior Warden, and Thomas Saunderson, Junior Warden, for opening the said Lodge, and for such further time only as shall be thought of by the brethren thereof. It being our will that this our appointment of the above officers, shall in no wise effect any future election of officers of said Lodge, and that such election shall be regulated agreeable to such By-laws of the said Lodge as shall be consistent with the

Grand Laws of the Society contained in the Book of Constitution. And we hereby will and require of you, the said Prince Hall, to take special care that all and every one of the said brethren are to have been regularly made Masons, and that they do observe, perform, and keep all the rules and orders contained in the Book of Constitution, and further that you do from time to time cause to be entered in a book kept for that purpose an account of your proceedings in the Lodge, together with all Rules, Orders and Regulations as shall be made for the Government of the same. That in no wise you omit in every year to send us or our successors, Grand Master, for the time being, an account of your said proceedings, and copies of all such Rules, Orders and Regulations as shall be made aforesaid, together with the list of the members of the Lodge, and such sums of money as may suit the circumstances of the Lodge and reasonably be expected toward the Grand Charity, "Moreover we will and require of you the said Prince Hall, as soon as conveniently may be, to send an account in writing of what may be done by virtue of these presents."

Given at London under our hand and seal of Masonry this 29th day of September, A. L. 5784, A. D. 1784, by the Grand Master's Command.

PETITION

Text of one of the many petitions sent to the General Court by **Prince Hall**, against slavery and slave trade, 1773-1778.

To the Honorable Council and House of Representatives for the State of Massachusetts Bay, in General Court assembled January 13th, 1777.

"The Petition of a great number of Negroes, who are detained in a state of Slavery, in the Bowels of a free and Christian Country-Humbly Shewing: "That your Petitioners apprehend that they have, in common with all other Men, a natural and unalienable right to that freedom, which the great Parent of the Universe hath bestowed equally on all mankind, and which they have never forfeited by any compact or agreement whatever. But they were unjustly dragged, by the cruel hand of power, from their dearest friends and some of them even torn from the embraces of their tender parents—From a populous, pleasant, and plentiful Country—and in violation of the Laws of nature and of nations and in defiance of all the tender feelings of humanity, brought together to be sold like beasts of burden and like them condemned to slavery for life. Among a people professing the mild Religion of Jesus . . . A people not insensible of the sweets of rational freedom nor without Spirit to resent the unjust endeavors of others to reduce them to a state of Bondage and subjection. Your Honors need not be informed that a life of Slavery—like that of your petitioners, deprived of every social privilege of everything requisite to render life even tolerable, is far worse than Non-Existence. In imitation of the laudable example of the good people of these States, your petitioners have long and patiently waited the event of petition after petition, by them presented to the Legislative Body of this State, and cannot but with grief reflect that their success has been but too similar. They cannot but express their astonishment, that it has never been considered that every principle from which America has acted in the course of her unhappy difficulties with Great Britain pleads stronger than a thousand arguments in favor of your petitioners. They therefore humbly beseech your Honors to give this petition its due weight and consideration and cause an Act of the Legislature to be passed whereby they may be restored to the enjoyment of that freedom which is the natural right of all men—and their children (who were born in this land of Liberty) may not be held as Slaves after they arrive at the age of twenty-one years. So many of the Inhabitants of this State (no longer chargeable with the inconsistency of acting, themselves, the part which they condemn and oppose in others) be prospered in their present glorious struggles for liberty; and have those blessings secured to them by Heaven of which benevolent minds cannot wish to deprive their fellowmen.

NEGRO FREEMASONRY AND SEGREGATION

And your Petitioners as in Duty bound shall ever pray—

PRINCE HALL,	Job Lock,
PETER BESS,	Jack X Peippont his mark
LANCASTER HILL,	Nero X Funilo his mark
BRISTER SLENFEN,	Newport X Summer his mark

THE COLOR LINE

No little speculation exists in the mind of the newly made Mason as to the status of Negro Freemasonry, so called. The fact that lodges made up of colored men, imitating and claiming to be Masons, using regalia and emblems copied from legitimate Freemasonry, are in existence, naturally excites a curiosity to know whence the American negro derived his alleged Freemasonry and what relationship, if any, it bears to that adopted and practiced by the white man.

The origin of Freemasonry among the negroes of the United States is as follows: On the sixth day of March, 1775, an army lodge chartered by the Grand Lodge of England attached to one of the regiments under General Gage stationed in Boston, Massachusetts, initiated Prince Hall and fourteen colored men of that city into the mysteries of the fraternity. From that beginning, with small additions from foreign countries, commenced Masonry among the negroes. It was the custom in those primitive days to permit brethren who were regularly made to assemble as a lodge, and the presumption is that the fifteen negroes who had received their Masonic degrees in the army body met as a lodge, but there is nothing to indicate that they did anything in the way of conferring degrees. On March 2, 1784, Prince Hall and his fourteen companions applied to the Grand Lodge or

England for a charter of warrant. This document was issued to them on September 29, 1784. They were given the designation of African Lodge No. 459, with Prince Hall as Master. For some reason, this charter was not received until May 2, 1787, nearly three years after its official date.

During the year 1919, members of the Mystic Shrine at Atlanta, Georgia, secured an injunction against certain colored men in that city, prohibiting them from using any of the signs, secret work, or appliances of that body. During the litigation, a copy of the old warrant issued to African Lodge No. 459 was brought into court from Baltimore, Maryland. It is reproduced in this discussion as a matter of general information:

Warrant of Constitution A.F.M.

To All and Every: Our right worshipful and loving brethren: We, Thomas Howard, Earl of Effingham, Lord Howard, etc., Acting Grand Master, under the authority of his Royal Highness, Henry Frederick, Duke of Cumberland, etc., Grand Master of the Most Ancient and Honorable Society of Free and Accepted Ancient Masons send greetings.

Know ye that we, at the humble petition of our Right Trusty and well beloved brethren, Prince Hall, Boston Smith, Thomas Sanderson, and several other brethren residing in Boston, New England, in North America, do hereby constitute the said brethren into a regular Lodge of Free and Accepted Masons, under the title or denomination of the African Lodge, to be opened in Boston, aforesaid, and do further at their said petition and of the great trust and confidence reposed in each of the said above named brethren, hereby appoint the said Prince Hall to be Master; Boston Smith, Senior Warden; and Thomas Sanderson, Junior Warden, for opening the said Lodge, and for such further time only as shall be thought by the brethren thereof, it being our will that this, our appointment of the above officers, shall in no wise affect any future election of officers of said Lodge, but that such election shall be regulated, agreeable to such By-Laws of the said Lodge as shall be consistent with the Grand Laws of the Society, contained in the Book of Constitutions; and we hereby will, and require of you, the said Prince Hall, to take special care that all and every, the said brethren, are to have been regularly made Masons, and that they do observe, perform, and keep all the rules and orders contained in the Book of Constitutions and further that you do from time to time cause to be entered in a book kept for that purpose, an account of your proceedings in the Lodge, together with all such rules, orders, and regulations as shall be made for the good government of the same; and in no wise you omit once in every year to send to us, or our successors, Grand Masters, or Rowland Holt, Esq., our Deputy Grand Master for the time being, an account of your said proceedings and copies of all such rules, orders and regulations as shall be made as aforesaid, together with the list of the members of the Lodge, and such sum of money as may suit the circumstances of the Lodge, and reasonably be expected toward the Grand Charity. Moreover, we will, and require of you, the Prince Hall, as soon as conveniently may be, to send an account in writing of what may be done by virtue of these presents.

Given at London, under our hand and seal of Masonry, this 29th day of September A.L. 5784 A.D. 1784 by the Grand Master's command."

African Lodge remained upon the English register until the union of the two rival Grand Lodges of Moderns and Ancients into the United Grand Lodge of England in the year 1813, when it was erased from the records because of its failure to contribute to the Charity Fund of the Grand Body.

But this by no means meant the elimination of Negro Masonry in the United States. Prince Hall was a man of more than usual ability. He worked zealously in the cause of Masonry and from 1792 until his death in 1807, he exercised all the functions of a provincial Grand Master. In 1797 he issued a license to thirteen black men, who had been made Masons in England to assemble and work as a lodge in Philadelphia. He also granted authority for the formation of a lodge in Providence, R. I. In 1808 these three lodges joined in forming African Grand Lodge, of Boston, now known as Prince Hall Grand Lodge of Massachusetts. The second colored Grand Lodge called the First Independent African Grand Lodge of North America for the Commonwealth of Pennsylvania was organized in 1815, and shortly after a third came into existence known as the Hiram Grand Lodge of Pennsylvania. In 1847, these three Grand Bodies fully recognized one another and joined in the formation of a National Grand Lodge, which has long since passed out of existence. Practically all negro lodges in the United States are descended from one or the other of the negro lodges, which were constituted by Prince Hall and later formed the various Grand Lodges which have already been spoken of.

Regardless of the apparent regular way and manner in which negro Masonry was introduced into the United States, the question of its legitimacy has been one widely discussed and over which there has been much controversy due largely to racial prejudice. The status of Negro Masonry in this country was perhaps never better defined than it was by Albert Pike in 1875, when he said, "Prince Hall Lodge was as regular a Lodge as any Lodge created by competent authority. It had a perfect right to establish other Lodges and make itself a Mother Lodge. I am not inclined to meddle in the matter. I took my obligations from white men, not from negroes. When I have to accept negroes as brothers or leave Masonry, I shall leave it. Better let the thing drift." This very frank state-

ment by Albert Pike sums up the exact feeling that is
exhibited toward Negro Masonry at the present time.

Certain objections to the legitimacy of Negro Masonry have been offered. But they are the complaints
of the prejudiced. The student who wants to know
the truth and is willing to weigh things impartially
must conclude that these objections are more in the
nature of excuses, and would never be brought forward were it not for the antithesis of race, which for
generations has divided the white man and the black
man and caused them to remain at a perpetual distance.

Among the most forcible objections which have
been offered is that the warrant by whose authority
Negro Masonry was formed was issued by a Grand
Lodge which had seceded from the Grand Lodge of
England and was known as The Ancients; that between the time of granting the warrant and delivery
of the same to African Lodge, the Grand Lodge of
Massachusetts had been formed thereby acquiring exclusive Masonic Jurisdiction over the territory in
which African Lodge was constituted; that it was illegal for the further reason that there was in Massachusetts a Provincial Grand Lodge of which General
Joseph Warren was Grand Master; that an examination of the charter issued to African Lodge discloses
no authority whatsoever permitting African Lodge to
admit anyone to its membership except Masons. No
authority was given in the warrant either to make

Masons or establish lodges and for this reason, when the lodge was erased from the roll by action of the Grand Lodge of England, colored Freemasonry in America forever ended.

On the other hand, some very distinguished and reliable Masonic writers have declared in all candor that African Lodge was just as legitimate as any lodge formed in the United States, and that therefore Negro Freemasonry is legitimate notwithstanding the existing prejudice which prohibits a recognition of that form of Masonry by the white man. It has been pointed out that African Lodge was warranted by the English Grand Lodge only as a lodge, and without any of the functions of a Grand Lodge and was, therefore, powerless to authorize the formation of other lodges. Yet there are abundant instances of where single lodges developed into Mother Lodges and numerous examples can be found in Europe and Asia where individual Masons on their own authority set up lodges which were afterwards universally accepted as legitimate. In our country Fredericksburg Lodge of Virginia was unable to furnish any claim to its existence as a chartered body, yet it had made George Washington a Mason and had organized a Lodge at Gloucester Court House.

This Lodge joined in the formation of the Grand Lodge of Virginia, and was accepted by that body as legitimate and regular.

NEGRO FREEMASONRY AND SEGREGATION

St. Andrew's lodge of Boston, Mass., received its charter from the Grand Lodge of Scotland in 1760, yet this lodge made Masons in 1753. In 1758 it gave to the Masonic world that illustrious Freemason, General Joseph Warren, who fell at Bunker Hill.

As to the careless manner of creating lodges and propagating Masonry which was so apparent in the beginning of the Eighteenth Century, George W. Speth of England, states that "throughout the last Century and well into this, lodges have been formed by British Masonry without previous consent or authority of the Grand Lodge or of the Grand Master. Neither have the founders of the Lodges been censured for their irregularity of conduct."

As to the claim that the formation of African Lodge was an invasion of rights of the Grand Lodge of Massachusetts, it is asserted that for several years there were two grand Lodges in England. New York, at one time, had three; South Carolina, two, so that the presence of two constituted authorities in a jurisdiction was not unusual because of the generally disorganized condition of Masonry in those early times and the lack of coordinated effort.

Concerning the objection which has been offered that the Negro Lodge rejected from its ritualistic formula the word "free-born" and inserted in its place the word "free," it is pointed out by the supporters of colored Masonry that the old Masonic documents from which Masonry draws much of its data and ritual

NEGRO FREEMASONRY AND SEGREGATION

makes use of the word "free," but not "free-born." It is also asserted that the Grand Lodge of England, in 1838, struck the word "freeborn" from its list and inserted the word "free," proving conclusively that the word "free-born" which appears in the ritual of Masonry, is not a fixed entity but has been made use of in accordance with the views of ritual builders from time to time. One of the strongest claims advanced against the legitimacy of colored Masonry is that the formation of Prince Hall Grand Lodge was in fact an ultimatum on the part of Negro Masonry to establish its own freedom and independence and in view of a protocol issued on the 18th day of June, 1827, its constituents publicly declared themselves free and independent of any lodge and declined to be governed by any body other than their own.

As we now understand the fraternity, this revival of colored Masonry and its assumption of Grand Lodge authority was illegal and from that day rendered the Prince Hall Grand Lodge and all its constituents as clandestine.

Regardless of the way and manner that Negro Masonry arose in America it is today regarded as spurious and illegitimate, a condition which will exist as long as human prejudice separates the white man and the black man.

(From: The History and Evolution of Freemasonry, By Delmar D. Darrah, Chicago, 1954.)

BLACKFACE: THE LODGES OF THE AMERICAN NEGRO

THERE IS no more instructive way to observe the impact of native culture upon an immigrant people than to inspect the lodges of the American Negro. A tour of such lodges would carry us from the United Brothers of Friendship and Sisters of the Mysterious Ten on down to the Grand United Order of the Fishermen of Galilee of the Eastern and Western Hemispheres, allowing us to pause for a moment in the sanctum of the Daughters of the Prairie of the Benevolent Protective Herd of Buffaloes of the World. And in this motley array, riotous and bedraggled, resounding with noisy words and moved by great, simple emotions, we should probably miss the tragedy of one race and the comedy of the other. We have made the Negro over in our own image and now we are laughing at him, but his imitation of our clubs only faintly parodies the originals, and the deftness with which he has seized and elaborated our tricks merely shows how primitive all of us are.

The total membership in sixty-odd Negro societies is approximately 2,500,000 and the property they own is probably in the neighborhood of $20,000,000. They have gone in for organization with a vengeance and with glee. Always deviled somewhat by finances, wearing in many cases regalia bought at bargain rates from white lodges that do not recognize them, they have few tangible achievements on their roster of success, yet these vast and picturesque bodies deserve their unit in the parade of the race.

1

High-minded whites began early to dress the Negro in symbolic robes and breeches. In 1693 Cotton Mather graciously laid down his *Rules for the Society of Negroes*. Every Sunday evening the slaves were allowed to assemble and pray together by turns. There was ceremony and the dim outlines of a Grand United Order back of these gatherings. One of the rules provided: "If any of our number shall fall into the Sin of *Drunkenness*, or *Swearing*, or *Cursing*, or *Lying*, or *Stealing*, or notorious *Disobedience*, or *Unfaithfulness* unto their Masters, we will *Admonish* him of his Miscarriage and forbid his coming to the Meeting, for at least *one* Fortnight." Other sins carried longer separation from the society's pleasures: "If any defile himself with Fornication, we will debar him from the Meeting at least *half a year*." What might be said to have corresponded to the ritual was the Catechism, which every member was required to learn. The duties incumbent upon members were clear: "If any of our fellow slaves should *Run Away* from their Masters, we will afford them *No Shelter*. But we will do what in us lies that they may be discovered, and punished. And if any *of us* are found Faulty, in this Matter, they shall no longer be *of us*."

To spread the cause of temperance among the colored, pious souls in 1847 organized the Independent Order of Good Samaritans and the Daughters of Samaria. There were trappings, dazzling regalia, emblems and all, cast for the Negro imagination, but the order ingeniously kept the Negro in his place. The state lodges, comprising the rulers, were white, and the district grand lodges were black. The Good Samaritans performed valiant deeds of service— among them, building an Asylum for Inebriates, to which the various lodges were entitled to send patients—but distressing breaches occurred. By 1881 there were three national branches, each claiming to be the right one. Two of these united, and the Negroes gradually gained ascendancy until, in 1887, they were able to elect a colored Grand Sire for the first time. This was too much—even for the prophet-eyed battalions of temperance—and the whites began to drop by the way. Now the Negroes have their sunburst of locals under such names as Crystal Fount, Rose of Sharon, Lily of the Valley, Good Intent, Ark of Safety, Neversink, Hand in Hand, Gassaway, Rising Star of the East, and, of course, Mt. Pisgah.

With all our moral ferocity, no reform among us has ever been able to command the sustained fellowship of white and black. In fact, questions of race have from the first embarrassed the pretensions of all the large brotherhoods. Odd Fellows, Masons, Knights of Pythias, and the Elks remain essentially Jim Crow. The Negroes, not content merely to be organized into bumfuzzling temperance bands, early put in a claim on these orders, but with only slight satisfaction. Albert Pike, high Masonic writer, said in 1868: "Freemasonry is one faith, one great religion, one great common star around which all men of all tongues and languages shall assemble." This same Pike shied on the approach of the Negro question, and said: "I took my obligation to white men, not to Negroes, and when I have to accept Negroes as brothers or leave Masonry, I shall leave Masonry." The official organ of the Grand Lodge of Kentucky of the Ancient and Honorable Society of Free and Accepted Masons asserts: "It can never be seriously contended that colored Masonry is more than an imitation of the higher Masonry of the whites."

Quaintly enough, it is the Negroes who are technical and the whites who are sentimental. The Negro claim of white Masonic fatherhood is based upon what they consider a truly accredited Negro lodge established in Boston by a Negro named Prince Hall in 1775. Hall was the son of an Englishman and a mulatto. He was an ordained Methodist minister and is said to have had a remarkable grasp on the Bible. Visiting members of a British lodge conferred degrees on Hall and fourteen of his fellows in Boston, and, feeling the importance of the honor, Hall and his followers set to work zealously to organize a lodge of full-fledged Masons. In 1789 the Grand Lodge of England granted a charter to the African Lodge in Boston. The Negro apologists point out that this lodge thus drew its charter from the Grand Lodge of England—the same source from which the charter of every early lodge of Masons in America was drawn. It is further argued and deposed by the champions of Negro Masonry that St. Andrew Lodge—the local which fought the Prince Hall Lodge and started rumors of illegality—was itself cloudy in origin and of doubtful regularity. The conclusion from the Negro point of view is that the Prince Hall Lodge was not only legal but that "its claim to legitimacy antedates that of the lodges of white men which questioned it."

Even if colored Masons have been kept to the buzzard roost, they have enjoyed the show. It is as if the play were written expressly for them—the windy titles, the long-bearded traditions, the hallowed conceits, and above all, the pleasure of guarding a vast treasure of wisdom so subtle as to be almost incommunicable. White Masonry has really denied itself the services of its most fluent exponents. William H. Grimshaw, a Negro Mason, declares:

> The great truths of Masonry heeded, constitute a security within and an impregnable fortress surrounding the human soul against which the weapons of evil will fall broken at our feet, and we are as little harmed as the atoms which dance in the sunbeams and nestle against our window panes.

Negroes accept with literal faith and touching naïveté the touchstone of Masonic philosophy. Its teachings are as real to them as Adam's rib, and if Masonry is *The Green Pastures* of the white race, it is likewise and intensely more the playground of the Negro's muscular imagination. Grimshaw gives the monthly payroll of the building of Solomon's Temple. Ethereal realities, too, yield to the open-eyed wonder and mystic contemplation of the Negro

mind. It is easy and delightful to see Brother Nathaniel
H. B. Cassell heaving up *Stones From the Quarries*, "being
an oration delivered on the occasion of St. John's Feast
Day, December 27th, A.D. 1915, Anno Lucis 5915 before
the Most Worshipful Grand Lodge of the Ancient Free
and Accepted Masons of Liberia." Here is pageantry and
drama, not your milk and water imitation of the sublime.
Hear him as he begins, "Most Worshipful Grand Master,
Right Worshipful Grand Wardens, Right Worshipful and
Worthy Officers and Brethren of the Mystic Tie, Elect
Sisters and Helpers near the Grand Establishment. . . ."
To "the twin-cherub of Christianity" the Negro has
brought the offerings of his faith, the rich gifts of musical
speech, and the aspirations of the common man for that
which is beyond and yet within him.

As a consequence, the white man can never deprive
the Negro of Masonry. He may be exiled, declared clandestine, and crossed with the bar sinister. But he holds on
to Masonry with the entreating clutch of love. Its spell has
fixed him immovably, and his devotion to Masonic ideals
has touched the white Mason if it has never abolished his
official frown. There are times when the Masonic spirit
leaps like fire from race to race. Among Negro Masons
there is a story which recounts how the Rev. D. R. Stokes,
a colored minister in Texas, dared years ago to speak out
against prohibition in the Lone Star State. Following his
address, he was taken in hand by a body of men who led
him across the Sabine River where they prepared to hang
him. As a last faint hope, Stokes is said to have given the
Masonic signal of distress. A ringleader caught the sign.
Immediately his demeanor changed. He became an advo-
cate of the black man whose body was already beginning
to stretch and after an earnest argument persuaded the
mob to untie its victim. This and other doubtless apocry-
phal yarns regale the Negro with pictures of his power and

the security of his fellowship. True or not, they reveal how completely he has accepted the banishment from white Masonry, without rancor or resentment, and yet clings to every trace of hope which will identify him with that august body.

The usual ascending scale of degrees attends Negro Masonry, culminating in both Scottish Rite and Knights Templar. This has made possible the Shrine, and here the Negro overshot himself with his usual generous love of mummery. One might think the Negro would be hard put to exceed in name and conception such a body as the Ancient Order of the Nobles of the Mystic Shrine for North America. Not at all. The Negroes assemble under the encircling banner of the Ancient Egyptian Arabic Order of the Nobles of the Mystic Shrine for North and South America. The Ancient Egyptian Arabic Order traces its apostolic succession as carefully as do the Negro Masons. It seems that Noble J. G. Jones and others received the mysteries from several members of the Shrine Council of Arabia when these members were visiting the Chicago World's Fair in 1893.

Regardless of how the Negro Shriners came by the ritual and pomp, they have been a dark-town strutters ball since they started. The Imperial Potentate's Report to the Thirteenth Annual Convention of the Imperial Council, held in Atlantic City, the Desert of New Jersey, Ramdam 12th, 13th, and 14th, Hegira 1329, announces that the Imperial Divan traveled by airplane from Chicago to Fort Worth and "dispensated Ruby Temple there." Hither and yon, the Imperial Potentate and his Divan go, dispensating. Medina Temple is in New York, Azure in Atlantic City, Fezzan at St. Paul, Mt. Sinai at Gulfport, Mississippi. The Courts of the Daughters of Isis are provided for the ladies of the members.

The Negro Shrine is often beset with the requests of

white Shriners who wish to visit its sessions. There are plenty of other troubles too. Nobles struggle to show themselves approved, but penury dulls their brilliance. Among items recorded in one report are: Cabs for officers, $34; One taxi for ladies, $2; Past Imperial Potentate's badge, $40. The Imperial Recorder announces that he is prepared to furnish a "full set of jewels of the Order for the sum of $10." He adds, however, that "no supplies will be furnished any Temple without cash." Among the assets listed for the Ancient Egyptian Arabic Order of the Nobles of the Mystic Shrine for North and South America are 700 unbound copies of the ritual, one desk and one typewriter.

One might suppose this to be all the long-suffering Masons could stand, but there is yet the Order of the Eastern Star Among the Colored People, with a membership of over 100,000. For obvious reasons the Eastern Star has been immensely in favor among Negro women. Both the indiscriminate sale of its ritual and the appeal of its exalted abracadabra to the Negro mind have carried it over. Consider the Queen of the South Degree. The officers and stations include King Solomon, Patron, in the East; Queen Bathsheba, Matron, on the right of Solomon; Princess Hattipha, Assistant Matron, in the West; and Princess Oziel, Conductress, in the South. At the door is a Warder on the inside and a Sentinel on the outside.

At the appointed hour, King Solomon takes his station in the East, calls the Palace to order with one resounding blow of his gavel, and says: "Princess Oziel, proceed to satisfy yourself that all who are within the audience-chamber are entitled to be present." Princess Oziel looks around officially and assures Most Excellent King Solomon that all are worthy. King Solomon next says to another dignitary: "Communicate with the Warder and command her vigilance to guard this Palace and preserve our deliberations from intrusion." Next King Solomon asks each of the officers the duties of her particular station, to which all make lofty answer. There follows a long argument over the rights of women to enjoy the secrets of divine truth, at the end of which King Solomon, who has been magnificently dubious all the while, is brought to taw. Read this ritual in what passes for Negro dialect and you will see why the Order of the Eastern Star has grown to such confounding proportions among the women who do the washing for those who make up the original.

2

What happened in Masonry has happened, if somewhat less elaborately, in Odd Fellowship. The white Odd Fellows, however, have not shown so much distress as the Masons over the Negro vulgarization of their beauties. For one thing, the Odd Fellows are not as the Masons in claiming to be the sentinels of an incomprehensible wisdom. For another, the legitimacy of colored Odd Fellowship is beyond question. Long before the War Between the States a Philomathean Institute, made up of freedmen, was formed in New York. The blacks of this institute applied to the Odd Fellows of their state for a charter, but their petition was haughtily refused. It happens that Peter Ogden, a Negro steward on the good ship *Patrick Henry*, heard of their rebuff. Ogden had been admitted to a lodge in England and he immediately took the matter up with the Grand Lodge of England, which granted a dispensation to the American Negro lodge in 1842. When the white lodges of America learned of the ruse, they withdrew from the Grand Lodge of England and formed the Independent Order of Odd Fellows.

The Negro branch carries the same name as its English parent, the Grand United Order of Odd Fellows. The sisters and wives of the Grand United Order form the Sojourna Household of Ruth, the purpose of which is to unite the women of Odd Fellowship "with their fathers, husbands, sons, and brothers in one great, happy, and prosperous family." All this must be accomplished on dues of 25 cents a month.

The Knights of Pythias of North and South America, Europe, Asia, and Africa continue the blackface performance among the big three. The Negro Knights made application for a charter at Richmond in 1869; they were refused, but some of the local Knights are said to have initiated the Negroes and the K.P.O.N.S.A.E.A.A. now number over 90,000 members, despite the fact that the white Pythians declare that "there are no Negro Knights of Pythias."

A fraternal benefit society with comfortable assets of $575,073, and distinct from the order just mentioned, is called the Colored Knights of Pythias. By shrewd management the Knights have shown that they belong, as they are recognized to be, among the sound insurance bodies of the Republic. A benefit membership of 10,834 is insured for $4,919,220. An endowment fund of $1,500,000 has been carefully accumulated and the body maintains a well-managed sanatorium at Hot Springs, Arkansas.

The Benevolent and Protective Order of Elks have been no more hospitable to the Negro than other large fraternal bodies, and for their pains they are thanked today by a ripsnorting band of 300,000 members among the colored people of the Improved Benevolent and Protective Order of Elks, with a chapter recently established amid considerable pomp in London, where Zulu singers were imported for the occasion. A porter on the Chesapeake and Ohio, Arthur J. Riggs, claimed to have "come in contact with enough workings" of the order to organize a lodge of Elks in Cincinnati in 1898. With the aid of B. F. Howard, he had the ritual copyrighted—a formality which the white lodges had overlooked, and there was nothing they could do to suppress the dusky rivals.

For a few years the pretensions of the Improved Order of Elks were overlooked, but in 1906, just before they were scheduled to meet in Brooklyn, the New York legislature passed a law forbidding the Negro to use the same emblem or call himself an Elk. There followed a disturbing division in the ranks of the Improved Order, which was never settled until 1909, when the two happily reunited. From steadfastly opposing them the white Elks have subsided into indifference and a policy of studiously ignoring their existence. This, however, appears not in the least to have affected the vigor of the Improved B.P.O.E. Their growth to importance has been steady, both in numbers and in concrete efforts on behalf of their race. They supplied the funds for the first survey of Negro health ever made in the United States. They have established a Goodwill Court in Harlem, where, through their efforts, something is being done to curb the appalling juvenile delinquency of that Mecca of the Negro. Last year they secured and engineered a performance of *The Green Pastures* in Washington exclusively for Negroes, who had been forbidden admission to the regular bill at the National Theatre there. When Negroes had persisted in attending the show, other patrons simply moved away, leaving a significant spread of "white space" about them. After prolonged negotiations the Elks got the management to rent the theater for an evening and Negroes were not only given a chance to see the epic of their own racial interpretation of white religion but also had the enviable chance of sitting anywhere they chose.

Other deeds equally meritorious are to the credit of the Improved Order of Elks, so that the name ceases to appear either comical or presumptuous. Their parades are a treat. In Washington, where the latest convention was held, there were 10,000 Elks in line. Colors of purple, white, and gold decked the streets for miles, with now and then a sprinkling of black, a dazzling array of flashing satin and silver. A unit from Philadelphia wore purple military uniforms and Haile Selassie helmets. A crack drill team from Boston strutted in satin trouserettes. Yet, even in this riotous spectacle, realism was not lacking. Swinging along the street came a detachment of nurses, carrying placards advertising Washington as the tuberculosis center of America.

During its years of greatest growth and expansion, the Improved Benevolent and Protective Order of Elks has had as its Grand Exalted Ruler J. Finley Wilson. He once ran a dance hall in Nevada with the late Tex Rickard, who lovingly called him Little Britches. Wilson's odyssey carried him through most of the states, as a porter, and later brought him back to Nevada and Tex. Now he owns the Washington *Eagle* and various other strong Negro newspapers, and enjoys the dignity of his office. A flashy dresser who carries a cane and smokes dreadnaught cigars, he has a marked penchant for flowery speeches, prize fights, and horse races, and a marked distaste for the routine entailed by his lofty office. If he did nothing to prevent it, he says, he would have as many as four appointments a day every day of the year.

3

By no means all Negro lodges stem from white fraternities. The United Brothers of Friendship and Sisters of the Mysterious Ten were organized in Louisville in 1861 by Negroes both free and slave. All the members were under age, but they knew how to run a lodge. By 1892 there were over 100,000 members, and Temples of the Sisters of the Mysterious Ten had been widely established. This lodge admitted whites, and from time to time some have availed themselves of its privileges.

NEGRO FREEMASONRY AND SEGREGATION

The International Order of Twelve or Knights and Daughters of Tabor began at Independence, Missouri, in 1872, exhibiting the most elaborate series of titles and ceremonials on display up to that time. The order claims to have grown out of an antislavery organization formed among Negroes in the South in 1846. The Knights meet in Temples and the Daughters in Tabernacles, "while as Princes and Princesses of the Royal House of Media, they convene for social and literary entertainments in Palatiums." Lower ranks, embracing Maids and Pages of Honor, meet in Tents. The symbolism of the International Order of Twelve is worked out around the cryptic meaning of the numbers 777 and 333.

The Grand United Order of Galilean Fishermen was founded in Washington in 1856. It claims Masonic origin and displays the sacred emblem of the fish, passion cross, rose, and other items of Scottish Rite Masonry. It achieved a membership of 56,000 by 1897, but shortly thereafter disaffection spread through the ranks. By 1904 there was an open break and 15 members suspended from the Galilean Fishermen because of disagreement over policies came together to found a separate body. Three New York Tabernacles were involved—North Star, Golden Key, Celestial. These three covenanted together. "Believing to better shield ourselves from the dangers at all times confronting us," the preamble to the new constitution ran, "and the more intelligently and efficiently to disseminate the good within us and eradicate the evil, it is right and essential that a combination of our several interests be had." Members resolved "to live in unity with one another and to love the world as best we can." After much discussion it was decided to adopt the name, Grand United Order of the Fishermen of Galilee of the Eastern and Western Hemispheres. Both this body and the Grand United Order of Galilean Fishermen are still active.

In 1881 the Rev. W. W. Brown hit upon the idea of teaching industry and thrift to his race through the mystic formulae and emblazoned paraphernalia of a secret society. Brown was born a slave in Georgia. He ran away as a boy and joined the Northern troops. After the war he was variously a jockey, a schoolteacher, a preacher, a temperance lecturer, and a race promoter. However, it was not until he established the Grand Fountain of the United Order of True Reformers that he came into his own. Behind a lodge of the most spectacular sort he instituted a shrewd financial plan. During the first 23 years the savings bank of the Grand Fountain brought its assets up to $500,000 and, with 10,000 depositors, had done a volume of business exceeding $10,000,000. A few years before Brown's death in 1897, the directors of the Grand Fountain paid him $50,000 for "the fruits of his genius," and Brown retired. The Grand Fountain played from Richmond, in its heyday at the beginning of the century employing an office staff of 104 and carrying on its work with enviable sobriety.

4

Regrettably, the Grand Fountain's model has not been followed in later organizations. Most Negro lodges are scrawny and pathetic, the height of their pretensions matched only by the depth of their impecuniosity. The Supreme Grand Chapter of the Order of the Eastern Star Among the Colored People will report $3.57 spent for stationery. The Manhattan Temple of the Daughters of the Elks of the World requires a monthly dues of 75 cents and provides that a member who owes more than $2.25 is "unfinancial and will not receive any benefits." Each member must also pay 10 cents annually—"known as a head tax." Cana Tabernacle of the Grand United Order of the Fishermen of Galilee has an initiation fee of $2, though a candidate may be admitted for as little as $1 if the Tabernacle so decrees. The monthly dues of the Martha Washington Chapter of the National Grand United Order of Brothers and Sisters of Love and Charity is 50 cents, and 30 days are allowed for the payment of fines and assessments. The Nora F. Taylor Lodge of the Forest of New York City, Grand United Order of Antelopes of America, is positively swank, asking an initiation fee of $10 and stating that half this amount must be paid in advance.

Sums ranging from $25 to $100 are paid from burial funds raised by the assessment of a death tax. Likewise, sick benefit insurance is paid in nominal amounts. If a member of Cana Tabernacle falls ill and is not in debt over $1.50, he or she receives $4 a week for the first six weeks and $2 a week for the second six weeks. The Sojourna Household of Ruth pays a similar amount, while the Nora F. Taylor Lodge of Antelopes allows $12 a week during the first six weeks and $6 a week for the second six weeks.

These benefits are necessarily hedged about by every conceivable regulation. If a member of the Manhattan Temple of the Daughters of the Elks of the World "shall become unfinancial, she shall appear in person and pay up her indebtedness and stand 90 days before she is benefited for aid." To be eligible for offices, "a member must be financial." The Martha Washington Chapter of the Brothers and Sisters of Love and Charity demands a doctor's certificate on a doctor's letterhead in case of illness. Virtually all these lodges announce that they will "not pay any member towards the increase of their family." All specify against female family sickness and sickness due to immoral causes.

If a member of the Sojourna Household of Ruth is reported sick and is caught drunk "or performing any description of work" while receiving benefits, the relief automatically stops. The Daughters of the Elks of the

World recently resolved that "only deceased members of
Manhattan Temple shall receive flowers, the same to be a
clock, not costing more than $10." The Daughters of the
Prairie of the Benevolent Protective Herd of Buffaloes of
the World visit a fine of 50 cents on those who refuse to
sit up with the sick, except in cases of contagious disease.

The violent family life of these lodges is shown in
their grisly by-laws. The Daughters of the Prairie pre-
scribe: "No member shall dictate to the Exalted Ruler."
In the Household of Ruth, "dictating to the Most Noble
Governor" is punished by a fine of not less than a dime or
more than a quarter. Any Antelope who attends a meeting
while intoxicated can be fined $2 for the first offense and
suspended for the second. The by-laws of the Antelopes
also rule against professional gambling, wife- or husband-
beating, and discussing the affairs of the order on the street.
Also: "Any member who shall conspire together to break
up or destroy any branch of this Order or shall willfully
disturb the peace or harmony of any meeting by use of
vile or violent language shall be fined $1.00 to $2.00 or
be suspended or expelled by vote of the Shelter."

No Fisherman of Galilee is allowed to speak more
than three times on a single subject or longer than five
minutes each time; "but in no case shall a member personally assail another." Insubordination draws a fine of
25 cents "and loss of voice and vote until the fine is paid."
It is well known that the Grand Matron and Grand Patron
of the Order of the Eastern Star Among the Colored
People often have at each other with the parliamentary
butcher knife. In some states the difficulty has gone so far
as the courts and resulted in rival Grand Chapters.

5

The irrepressible Negro fancy has managed to make
it a matter of some importance that he must band together

with his fellows in penurious relief associations. His inveterate love of ceremony has given magnificence to his rags. He enters the lodge doors with his eyes closed, only to open them upon a world of pomp and circumstance as real to him as the rent. The emblems of his lodge are amulets around his neck. One of the symbols of the Order of the Sons and Daughters of Samaria, for example, is a triangle with a dove and an olive leaf enclosed. This is "emblematical of a peaceful life surrounded by dangers, and as it was a token with Noah that dry land was in the distance, just so doth it remind us that we are passing through the storms of life, surrounded with difficulties and overwhelmed in a sea of trouble. . . ." Yet land is not far and the triangle is the protection of the brotherhood. The gavel "symbolizes an instrument which may be used to subdue passions."

Every lodge is organized into a heavenly array of officers and its business is conducted in the grand manner. The Order of the Eastern Star has its International Grand Adah, Esther, Martha, and Sentinel. All the officers of the Grand Lodge of the Grand United Order of the Fishermen of Galilee are Grand This-and-that, including Orator, Conductress, Inside and Outside Guards, and Organizer. The Grand Organizer gets $10 from headquarters every time he establishes a new Tabernacle. The Grand Orator details any difficult point of law and gets traveling expenses to and from the Grand Lodge. The Grand Chaplain has charge "of the Holy Bible and candlesticks during the Grand Session." The Sojourna Household of Ruth has its Past Most Noble Governor, its Worthy Shepherd, Worthy Prelate, Worthy Usher, and so on. Inmates, as the members are called, must salute the Most Noble Governor upon entering or retiring from the chamber of proceedings. They must also wear a rosette badge of pink and white to all meetings.

NEGRO FREEMASONRY AND SEGREGATION

It is fitting that such dignitaries and their minions should be properly regaled. On this point the Negro will brook no trifling. A brother or sister is allowed to turn out with the Fishermen of Galilee only in the regulation uniform and dress. The annual sermon is a feature occasion in all lodges. The Fishermen appoint the second Sunday in November as anniversary day and command that "all lodges shall secure some place of worship, and give thanks to God for their perpetual existence."

The dress parade orders which the Antelopes must observe when attending the annual sermon are: for females, a one-piece white dress with long sleeves, brown gloves, a fez with a gold tassel, and the lodge emblem, for males, a dark suit, brown gloves, brown fez, and badge. The badges are so designed that at funerals they may be worn "with the mourning side out." The by-laws of the Daughters of the Prairie state that regulation dress "shall be white, compulsory"; moreover, "any member failing to wear white, whether in mourning or not, shall be fined the sum of twenty-five cents, payble at the moment."

With so much white in evidence, it is a relief to know that the highest degree bestowed by the Fishermen of Galilee is the Black Degree and the color for the lowest is white. In all cases there is a strict provision, with expulsion as the penalty, for wearing the regalia of the lodge outside of meeting hours or on the streets at any time other than the duly prescribed occasions of state.

6

These lodges are an effort not so much to escape life as to embellish it; there is sadness in every preamble. The Daughters of the Prairie state as their object, "the elevation of character, the relief of suffering humanity, by helping to care for our Sick and bury our Dead . . . trusting there will be adherence to said rules, which will cultivate a solid principle."

Young Negro intellectuals complain that lodges do next to nothing. Entranced members spend money on ceremonial costumes and squander time on conventions, parades, and burials. These keep the Negro from his work and exhaust his slender savings if he is not already impoverished. More insidious still, say the critics, is the fact that the lodges are hardly more than makeshift affairs, enlisting a blind devotion to elusive and impractical ideals, and thus deflecting progress and standing in the way of more substantial organizations for the improvement of the Negro's lot.

Be that as it may, the glory of the lodge remains un-dimmed in the eyes of its members. It is a sanctuary which the Negro himself has created. "The reason these fraternal meetings last so late at night," said one leader, "is that all week the colored man, in his job under the white man, has had little things that make him mad and that he can't talk out loud about. These things bile up inside of him." In the sacred chambers of the Grand United Order of the Fishermen of Galilee of the Eastern and Western Hemispheres, or under any other banner which invokes a sense of transcendent power, the Negro has his innings.

Enslaved by a freedom for which they were not prepared, distraught and belabored by a society at once hostile and patronizing, history displays nothing remotely equal to the progress the Negro has made in commerce and art. Yet, regardless of what Negroes do or how well they do it, they will remain alien for a hundred years to come. No one can know how true this is until he has walked through Harlem on a winter night; and after he has seen the children of African tribes shivering in stone cages, he can never really doubt it.

The Negro lodges are, then, the shelter of a badgered

NEGRO FREEMASONRY AND SEGREGATION

race. Their extravagant names are not far from weird jungle cries. Forced by conceit and discrimination to earn their living from the menial tasks of society, the Negroes face an incessant struggle with insecurity and want. Their answer is the Brothers and Sisters of Love and Charity. In slavery their refuge was a song; today it is a lodge.

(From: 50,000,000 Brothers, By Charles W. Ferguson, New York, 1937; by permission of Rinehart & Co., Publishers.)

REPORT ON NEGRO FREEMASONRY BY THE M.W. GRAND LODGE OF MASSACHUSETTS

At a regular Quarterly Communication of the Grand Lodge of Masons in Massachusetts held March 12, 1947, it considered a fact-finding report made by a committee of six Past Grand Masters concerning Negro Freemasonry in Massachusetts. The report was accepted, approved and recorded by unanimous vote of the Grand Lodge. The Committee did not recommend, and the Grand Lodge did not vote, what is Masonically known as "recognition." Neither was any action taken concerning intervisitation.

So many questions have been asked, and so many mis-statements have been made about the action of the Grand Lodge, that I am directed by the Most Worshipful Grand Master to disseminate a full copy of the official Minutes of that meeting, so far as they relate to Negro Freemasonry. This copy will be found on the following pages.

Fraternally yours
Frank H. Hilton,
Grand Secretary

NEGRO FREEMASONRY AND SEGREGATION

On January 24, 1947, by the order of Most Worshipful Grand Master Samuel H. Wragg, I caused the following letter to be sent to each voting member of the Grand Lodge, as well as to each Lodge Secretary:

JANUARY 24, 1947

Dear Brother:

The Most Worshipful Grand Master, on March 22, 1946, appointed the following named Brethren, all Past Grand Masters, as a committee to investigate the subject of Negro Freemasonry and to report to him:

M.W. Joseph Earl Perry, Chairman
" Melvin M. Johnson
" Arthur D. Prince
" Claude L. Allen
" Albert A. Schaefer
" Arthur W. Coolidge

Enclosed herewith is a copy of the unanimous report of this committee, as read to the Grand Lodge by the Grand Master at the regular Quarterly Communication on December 11, 1946.

Action on the acceptance of this report and the adoption of the recommendations will be taken at the regular Quarterly Communication of the Grand Lodge on March 12, 1947.

That all members of the Grand Lodge may have full opportunity to consider this report before action will be taken, a copy is being sent to each voting member of Grand Lodge as well as to each Lodge Secretary.

Fraternally yours
FRANK H. HILTON
Grand Secretary

NEGRO FREEMASONRY AND SEGREGATION

November 25, 1946

To the Most Worshipful Grand Master of Masons in Massachusetts:

The Committee appointed by you to consider and report on the subject of Negro Freemasonry in Massachusetts, begs leave to submit the following report:

It has been a full half century since our Grand Lodge has considered the subject of Negro Freemasonry. Then, and in all previous studies of the subject, attention was directed primarily, if not solely, to the question of the technical regularity of the origins and early history of Negro Freemasonry. In the light of the evidence then available, it was believed that it could not, according to Masonic Law, be regarded as legitimate Freemasonry. On the same evidence the same conclusions would presumably have been reached — and perhaps even more emphatically — if the individuals and lodges in question had been white instead of colored.

In the intervening half century, Masonic historical research has made much progress, and the emphasis has changed considerably in Masonic thinking with respect to some of the factors involved in any such inquiry. The legality and regularity of each organizational act is now tested according to the law and customs of its date rather than by those of the present.

Your Committee finds that according to the then prevailing Masonic law and custom, the origin, early procedures and subsequent development of the so-called Prince Hall (Negro) Freemasonry in this Commonwealth have been, and are, regular and legitimate. Moreover, there is reliable and uncontradicted documentary evidence, dated June 30, 1784, that African Lodge, of which Prince Hall was Master, was, in 1776, granted a "Permet" by John Rowe of Boston (then Provincial Grand Master over North America where no other Provincial was appointed), "to walk on St. John's day and Bury our dead in form," etc. Rowe became Provincial Grand Master in 1768.

NEGRO FREEMASONRY AND SEGREGATION

Thus for 170 years African Lodge and its successors have been functioning in Massachusetts in good faith and with the justifiable belief that their origin and procedure were as regular and legitimate as we have thought ours to be. Obviously, we do not presume to pass upon conditions prevailing in any other jurisdictions.

It is understood that there are other groups of Negroes who claim to be Masons but we have found no evidence in support of such claims, and our conclusion thus far is that the so-called Prince Hall (Negro) Freemasonry is, alone, entitled to any claim of legitimacy among Negroes in this Commonwealth.

Members of this Committee have inspected the original charter of African Lodge, No. 459, granted by authority of H.R.H. the Duke of Cumberland, Grand Master of our own Mother Grand Lodge of England, dated 29th September, 1784, appointing Prince Hall (a Negro resident of Boston) to be its Master. This is the source of all "duly constituted" Prince Hall Freemasonry, and is now in the possession of the M.W. Prince Hall Grand Lodge, F. & A.M. of Massachusetts. Our Grand Lodge traces its history as a "duly constituted" organization to 1733, and Prince Hall (Negro) Freemasonry to 1787 when African Lodge began to function under its Charter. Thus for more than a century and a half, these two branches of Freemasonry have existed side by side in this Commonwealth, each by its own preference adhering strictly to its own racial sphere of activity and without intervisitation.

There is need for unifying and strengthening all influences for the improvement and uplifting of mankind. Freemasonry seeks to build character and promote brotherhood among all men. These objectives have nothing to do with race or color or social or economic status. In this country, the welfare and the future of the white and colored people are interdependent and largely identical. Each has its own schools and colleges and churches and societies, but both have the same ultimate hopes and aspirations; both make common sacrifices in defense of their single country; both read the same periodicals, hear the

NEGRO FREEMASONRY AND SEGREGATION

same radio programs, and enjoy or suffer together the triumphs or failures of our national well being; and each is affected by the material and spiritual welfare of the other.

In conclusion, your Committee believes that in view of the existing social conditions in our country, it is advisable for the official and organized activities of white and colored Freemasons to proceed in parallel lines, but organically separate and without mutually embarrassing demands or commitments.

However, your Committee believes that, within these limitations, informal cooperation and mutual helpfulness between the two groups upon appropriate occasions are desirable.

Your Committee makes no recommendation except that this report be accepted, approved and recorded.

Fraternally submitted

JOSEPH EARL PERRY, Chairman	CLAUDE L. ALLEN
MELVIN M. JOHNSON	ALBERT A. SCHAEFER
ARTHUR D. PRINCE	ARTHUR W. COOLIDGE

Most Worshipful Joseph Earl Perry, Chairman of the Committee, then made the following motion:

Most Worshipful:

I move that the report of our Committee as read by you be accepted, approved and recorded. In so doing, I think it appropriate to say that your Committee of Past Grand Masters had relatively little difficulty in agreeing as to the legitimacy of Prince Hall Freemasonry, but did encounter some real perplexities when it came to phrasing their conclusions, for they felt that the subject matter is potentially controversial and that a wrong emphasis, however well intended, might harm the very ones whose interests we have at heart.

After our preliminary discussions, therefore, I submitted to the Committee several drafts of possible reports to serve as starting points for our further discussions, the several reports varying primarily in the degree to which it seemed wise to go in the proposed official action. The Committee selected the one which you have just read and made its further amendments and refinements on that framework. It may not satisfy those of our members who believe we should go the full distance toward complete intervisitation or those at the other extreme who believe we should do nothing, but your Committee is of the opinion that at this time, the Grand Lodge should do no less, and could not wisely do more, than is suggested in the report.

The work of the Committee was promptly attended to, but we have purposely deferred official presentation to the Grand Lodge for nearly a year, during most of which time discussion of the subject matter has been systematically carried on throughout the jurisdiction and copies of the Committee report containing its recommendations have been sent to each voting member of the Grand Lodge and have also been furnished to all who have made inquiries. Whatever action may be taken on this motion may, therefore, be deemed to represent the considered judgment of our entire membership as represented by the Grand Lodge.

Prior to any action being taken, Most Worshipful Melvin M. Johnson spoke of his long interest in the subject matter, outlined the early history of Negro Freemasonry in this country, answered such questions or objections to the action proposed by the Committee as he had encountered, and outlined his reasons for believing in the importance and timeliness of action at this time.

He first called attention to the fact that the Committee does not recommend what is technically known Masonically as "recognition." Neither does it recommend intervisitation. Mere acknowledgement of legitimacy implies neither.

The following is a summary of his address pertaining to the early history and development of Negro Freemasonry in Massachusetts:

There exists in the United States a completely organized and functioning Masonic world of which many of us know little, although it descends directly from the Mother Grand Lodge of the world, that of England.

NEGRO FREEMASONRY AND SEGREGATION

I refer to the Negro Freemasonry which, in order to distinguish it from the Freemasonry of our own technical recognition, has been differentiated by itself as of "Prince Hall Affiliation." One out of every eight Freemasons in the United States belongs to its bodies, which are as legitimate and as regular and duly-constituted as our own.

Some years ago, supposing that Negro Freemasonry was clandestine or at least irregular, I began the writing of a brief to prove it. In preparation therefor, I searched for and studied all known facts which were pertinent, seeking the best evidence. The result, much to my surprise, was a firm conviction of the genuineness of Prince Hall (Negro) Freemasonry. The facts and law are so clear that, in my opinion, no unbiased searcher for the truth can come to a different conclusion. I did not finish my study until the fall of 1944 and did not suggest its consideration in this Grand Lodge until after it had been discussed by the Grand Master of Masons in Oregon at the Grand Masters' Conference in Washington in 1946. It then seemed wise to bring it to the attention of our own Grand Master and Grand Lodge.

African Lodge No. 1

On March 6, 1775, a freeman by the name of Prince Hall, and fourteen other free colored men, were initiated in Boston by Army Lodge No. 441 of the Irish Constitution.

The claim has been made that an Irish military Lodge had no right to initiate civilians. From 1768, that was the Irish rule where, and only where, there was an Irish "Town Lodge." There was none such in Boston. Even if there had been, it would not have affected the status of a candidate although the Lodge which violated the rule might have been punished. There was no such English rule until 1815.

On July 3, 1776, African Lodge No. 1 was organized in Boston by an assembly of unaffiliated Negro Brethren and authority from that Army Lodge. (In almost identical fashion, Union Lodge of Albany, now Mount Vernon Lodge No. 3, under the

NEGRO FREEMASONRY AND SEGREGATION

Grand Lodge of New York, was born.) Its "Regulations" (By-Laws) were adopted January 14, 1779.

There were then no independent Grand Lodges in the whole of the Western Hemisphere. Moreover, there were then only five Provincial Grand Lodges which, with their descendants, persist today, viz: Massachusetts (2), Georgia, South Carolina and Pennsylvania.

Official acknowledgment of the legitimacy of African Lodge No. 1 was almost immediately made by John Rowe of Boston, Provincial Grand Master for North America, holding authority from the premier Grand Lodge of the world, that of England. He issued a permit authorizing the Lodge to appear publicly as a Masonic body in procession for the purpose of celebrating the Feast of Saint John and to bury its dead.

On both March 2 and June 30, 1784, African Lodge No. 1 applied to the Grand Lodge of England for a charter. This is the same Grand Lodge which, through Henry Price as Provincial Grand Master, founded the first "duly constituted" Freemasonry in the Western Hemisphere in 1733. On September 29, 1784, a charter was executed for African Lodge No. 459 by authority of the Duke of Cumberland, then Grand Master of our Mother Grand Lodge of England.

This was not a trespass for an owner cannot trespass upon property of which he is already in possession. It is true that the Massachusetts Grand Lodge (of Scottish origin) assumed its independence March 8, 1777. (1 Mass. 259) However, the St. John's Grand Lodge functioning by authority of the Grand Lodge of England under Provincial Grand Master John Rowe, continued as such until after his death in February, 1787. (1 Mass. 220) It first assumed authority to act as an independent Grand Lodge on July 29, 1790, when it elected John Cutler as Grand Master. (1 Mass 221) Thus it will be seen that at the time when the charter of African Lodge No. 459 was granted, as well as when the Lodge was organized on May 6, 1787, the Grand Lodge of England was still exercising its authority over the territory where African Lodge was established. Twice

African Lodge had sent the fee due to the Grand Lodge of England for its charter and twice the money failed to reach the Officers of the Grand Lodge of England. Finally, on March 10, 1787, the charter was paid for and delivered to Captain Scott, the third messenger and son-in-law of John Hancock.

On May 6, 1787, African Lodge No. 459 was formally organized in Boston under the charter, with Prince Hall as Worshipful Master. That charter is in existence today in a safe deposit vault in the City of Boston, Massachusetts, and has been inspected by members of your Committee. There is no question of its authenticity. Moreover, it is believed to be the only original charter issued from the Grand Lodge of England which is now in possession of any Lodge in the United States.

May 18, 1787, a list of members of this Lodge showed eighteen Masters, four "Crafts" and eleven Entered Apprentices. Twenty-three of the names on the list are not of the original fifteen.

African Lodge thereafter functioned as a Mother Lodge; that is to say, it assumed authority to establish other Lodges much as, indeed, it had itself been founded by the Irish Army Lodge in 1776.

Where Grand Lodges exist, the chartering of new Lodges by other existing Lodges would not be recognized today. It, however, was common in the Eighteenth Century, as every Masonic historian knows. In other words, at the time African Lodge functioned as a Mother Lodge, what it did was then a lawful practice of the Fraternity.

Some have believed that the Grand Lodge of England later revoked or annulled the charter of African Lodge. Such is not the fact. It is correct that at the union of 1813, the Grand Lodge of England revised its roll of particular Lodges and omitted those which had gone out of existence or become attached to some other Grand Lodge. This had no effect upon the legitimacy or standing of any erased Lodge. Some seventy Lodges located in the United States, which had at some time been carried on the English roll, were dropped from the roll in revisions. African Lodge, No. 459 (later No. 370) was one of them. So was St. John's Lodge then and now of Boston, constituted in 1733, the oldest Lodge of continuous existence in all the Americas.

Prince Hall Grand Lodge

African Grand Lodge (1791) was organized by an assembly of the Craft. The same method was used by the Moderns (1717), and the Antients (1751) in England; likewise by New Jersey (1787) in the United States. Two additional Lodges were established by African Lodge in 1797: African Lodge of Philadelphia and Hiram Lodge No. 3 of Providence. In 1808, after Prince Hall's death, a delegate convention of the three existing Lodges changed the name to "Most Worshipful Prince Hall Grand Lodge, F. and A.M." as a memorial to him. Note that the 1791 Grand Lodge was organized the year before our own present united Grand Lodge. At that time, there were functioning with their See at Boston, Massachusetts, St. John's Grand Lodge (English, 1733–1792), Massachusetts Grand Lodge (Scottish, 1769–1792), and the Lodge of St. Andrew, working independently.

In 1791, when this first Negro Grand Lodge was organized, there were only eleven other existing Grand Bodies of Symbolic Freemasonry in the whole Western Hemisphere which today exist. They were located in Massachusetts, Virginia, Maryland, Pennsylvania, Georgia, New Jersey, New York, South Carolina, North Carolina, Connecticut and New Hampshire. The Grand Lodge of Rhode Island was organized the next day. (1915 Mass. 281-2) This Negro Grand Lodge was not organized with any prescribed territorial jurisdiction. Like the present York Grand Lodge in Mexico, its "jurisdiction" was not territorial, but was limited to a certain class; the Prince Hall Grand Lodge to negroes and the York Grand Lodge to English speaking residents of Mexico.

NEGRO FREEMASONRY AND SEGREGATION

It has been urged and is still believed by many that the formation of African Lodge No. 1 and of its successor, African Lodge No. 459, violated the doctrine of "exclusive territorial jurisdiction."

Often an existing rule of law is wrongly cited to show the illegality of something which took place before that rule was established. Whatever effect the doctrine of "exclusive territorial jurisdiction" may have, it cannot be rightfully used to render illegal that which existed legally before the doctrine was asserted. Neither can it be used effectively where estopped by the equitable doctrines of laches or stale demands. Indeed, the Constitutions of our own Grand Lodge make an exception to that doctrine wherever territorial jurisdiction is "shared with another Grand Lodge by mutual consent" (Section 712). It has shared that jurisdiction in Massachusetts with the Prince Hall Grand Lodge for a century and a half by that silence which tacitly gave consent. Such sharing does not destroy the doctrine of territorial jurisdiction, but, rather, affirms it.

Massachusetts has three Lodges in Chile, founded in 1853, 1876 and 1884, respectively, and yet we recognize and exchange Representatives with the Grand Lodge of Chile.

At the present time, we recognize the York Grand Lodge of Mexico, which claims jurisdiction over English-speaking people in the whole of Mexico, and we also recognize Mexican Grand Lodges with concurrent territorial jurisdictions. In China, we have maintained Lodges of our obedience since 1863, and yet we have acted in comity there for many years with Lodges of the obedience of the Grand Lodges of England, Scotland, Ireland, Austria and the Philippines.

In the Canal Zone and Panama, the Grand Lodges of Massachusetts and Panama share certain limited territorial jurisdiction with each other by treaty. (1917 Mass. 79 and 1921 Mass. 141)

It is true that the Provincial Grand Lodge of Henry Prince and its successor have functioned continuously since 1733.

NEGRO FREEMASONRY AND SEGREGATION

It is also true, however, that there never has been a moment since November 30, 1756 (the date when the Grand Lodge of Scotland chartered the Lodge of St. Andrew in Boston) when there has not been a sharing of lawful Symbolic Freemasonry functioning in what is now the Commonwealth of Massachusetts. Before the evacuation of Boston, there were various Army Lodges functioning here, under charters from the Grand Lodges of England, Scotland and Ireland. The Lodge of St. Andrew continued after the union of 1792 to operate under its Scottish charter until 1809, when it united with this Grand Lodge. From December 27, 1769, until December 6, 1782, the Lodge of St. Andrew was a part of the Provincial Grand Lodge established by Scotland and known as the Massachusetts Grand Lodge, of which Brother Joseph Warren was Provincial Grand Master. This Scottish Provincial Grand Lodge declared itself independent on December 6, 1782. Meanwhile, the English Provincial Grand Lodge of 1733, then known as St. John's Grand Lodge, and the Massachusetts Grand Lodge continued to function as separate Grand Lodges in this Commonwealth until 1792, when these two Grand Lodges united, since which time in White Freemasonry there has been but one Grand Lodge. * * * * * * Assuming that our Grand Lodge has rightfully had and now has exclusive Masonic jurisdiction over Massachusetts, then we certainly have the right to allow another Grand Lodge to share that jurisdiction to such extent as we see fit.

It is somewhat interesting to note that although our Grand Lodge has been a party to proceedings in court to establish the illegitimate character of a number of irregular and clandestine operations, claiming to be Masonic, yet it never has proceeded against Prince Hall Freemasonry. In fact, in one criminal case prosecuted against clandestine Negro Freemasonry by the Prince Hall Grand Lodge, our then Grand Secretary testified as a witness against the clandestine outfit.

Other super-technical claims of the irregularity of Prince Hall Freemasonry have been made, none of which is sufficiently important from a legalistic viewpoint to require comment. The real opposition to Negro Freemasonry is rather social than legal. A vast majority of the Grand Lodges of the world outside of the United States and Canada, recognized by us, have Negro members as legitimate as ourselves and I have sat with them on quite a number of occasions when visiting in foreign countries. Their test is culture, not color. Even in Massachusetts, there is one authenticated instance of a Negro who, by reason of his office in his particular Lodge, was a member of and had a vote in this Grand Lodge. In 1867, a Bishop of the Episcopal Church and the Negro caterer to the Grand Lodge knelt together at the Altar of one of our oldest and most highly respected Lodges to receive their Masonic obligation. It is so recorded. In my mother Lodge, I have sat with Negro visitors who were members of legitimate English Lodges.

There are some who say, "Why do anything?" The fundamental answer is that we should practice our own teachings. Moreover, there is need of leadership in this day when, in the words of Bishop Pardue, "The clash between the application of a democratic philosophy and vast racial discrimination, is daily making new converts to the religion of communism."

(For documentation, see printed Proceedings of St. John's Grand Lodge, Massachusetts Grand Lodge and Grand Lodge of Masons in Massachusetts; also *A History of Freemasonry Among Negroes in America* by Harry E. Davis, 1946, which cites original sources of information.)

Acceptance of the report of the Committee and the adoption of the recommendations were unanimously voted by the Grand Lodge.

A true copy of the record.

Attest: Frank H. Hilton,
                                                        Grand Secretary

From: Report on Negro Freemasonry, March 12, 1947; The Grand Lodge of Massachusetts.)

TOLERATION

Masonry is the handmaid of religion. The Brahmin, the Jew, the Mahometan, the Catholic, the Protestant—each professing his peculiar religion, sanctioned by the laws, by time, and by climate—may retain their faith, and yet may be Masons.

Masonry teaches, and has preserved in their purity, the cardinal tenets of the old primitive faith, which underlie and are the foundation of all religions. Masonry is the universal morality which is suitable to the inhabitants of every clime—to the man of every creed. It has taught no doctrines except those truths that tend directly to the well-being of man; and those who have attempted to direct it toward useless vengeance, political ends, the Kabala, Hermeticism, Alchemy, Templarism, and Jesuitism, have merely perverted it to purposes foreign to its pure spirit and real nature.

The best, and, indeed, the only good Mason, is he who, with the power of labor, does the work of life—the upright mechanic, merchant, or farmer—the man who exercises the power of thought, of justice, or of love—whose whole life is one great act of performance of Masonic duty. The natural work of Masonry is practical life: the use of all the faculties in their proper spheres and for their natural functions. Love of truth, justice, and generosity, as attributes of God, must appear in a life marked by these qualities. The natural form of Masonry is goodness, morality, living a true, just, affectionate, self-faithful life, from the motive of a good man. It is loyal obedience to God's law. The good Mason does that which is good, which comes in his way, from a love of duty; and not merely because a law enacted by man or God commands his will to do it. Not in vain does the poor or oppressed look up to him. You find such men in all Christian sects, Protestant and Catholic; in all the great religious parties of the civilized world—among Buddhists, Mahometans, and Jews. They are kind fathers, generous citizens, and unimpeachable in their business: you see their Masonry in their works and in their play. The true Mason loves not only his kindred and his country, but all mankind; not only the good, but also the evil among his brethren. Though the ancient and honorable of the earth bid him bow down to them, his stubborn knee bends only at the bidding of his manly soul. His Masonry is his freedom before God, not his bondage unto men.

The old theologies, the philosophies of religion of ancient times, will not suffice us now; there are errors to be made way with, and their places supplied with new truths, radiant with the glories of heaven. There are great wrongs and evils in Church and State, in domestic, social, and public life, to be righted and outgrown. Masonry cannot in our age forsake the broad way of life; she must journey on in the open street, appear in the crowded square, and teach men by her deeds—her life—more eloquent than any lips.

It teaches Toleration, and inculcates in the strongest manner that great leading idea of the Ancient Art—that a belief in the one true God, and a moral and virtuous life, constitute the only religious requisites needed to enable a man to be a Mason.

It has ever the most vivid remembrance of the terrible and artificial torments that were used to put down new forms of religion or extinguish the old. It sees with the eye of memory the ruthless extermination of all the

people, of all sexes and ages—because it was their mis-
fortune not to know the God of the Hebrews, or to worship him under the wrong name—by the savage troops of
Moses and Joshua. It sees the thumbscrews and the
racks; the whip, the gallows, and the stake; the victims
of Diocletian and Claverhouse; the miserable covenan-
ters; the non-conformists; Servetus bound, and the unof
fending Quaker hung. It sees Cranmer hold his arm,
now no longer erring, in the flame, until the hand drops
off, in the consuming heat. It sees the persecutions of
Peter and Paul, the martyrdom of Stephen, the trials
of Ignatius, Polycarp, Justin, and Irenaeus; and then,
in turn, the sufferings of the wretched Pagans under the
Christian emperors, as of the Papists in Ireland, and
under Elizabeth and the besotted Henry; and all that in
all ages have suffered by hunger and nakedness, peril
and prison, the rack, the stake, and the sword—it sees
them all, and shudders at the long roll of human atroci-
ties.

Man never had the right to usurp the unexercised prerogative of God, and condemn and punish another for his
belief. Born in a Protestant land, we are of that faith:
if we had opened our eyes to the light under the shadows
of St. Peter's at Rome, we should have been devout Ro-
manists; born in the Jewish quarter of Aleppo, we should
have contemned Christ as an imposter; in Constantin-
ople, we should have cried, ''Allah il Allah—God is great,
and Mahomet is his Prophet.'' Birthplace and education
give us our faith.

Few believe in any religion because they have examined the evidences of its authenticity, and made up a
formal judgment, upon weighing the testimony. Not one
in ten thousand knows anything about the proofs of his
faith. We believe what we are taught; and those are

most fanatical who know least of the evidences on which their creed is based.

What is truth to me is not truth to another. The same arguments and evidences that convince one mind, make no impression on another: this difference is in men at their birth. No man is entitled positively to assert that he is right, where other men, equally intelligent and equally well-informed, hold directly the opposite opinion. Each thinks it impossible for the other to be sincere; and each, as to that, is equally in error. "What is truth?" was a profound question—the most suggestive one ever put to man. Many beliefs of former and present times seem incomprehensible. They startle us with a new glimpse into the human soul—that mysterious thing, more mysterious the more we note its workings. Here is a man, superior to myself in intellect and learning, and yet he sincerely believes what seems to me too absurd to merit confutation; and I cannot conceive, and sincerely do not believe, that he is both sane and honest; and yet, he is both. His reason is as perfect as mine, and he is as honest as I am.

The fancies of a lunatic are realities to him. Our dreams are realities while they last; and in the past, no more unreal than what we have acted in our waking hours. No man can say that he hath as sure possession of a truth as of a chattel.

When men entertain opinions diametrically opposed to each other, and each is honest, who shall decide which hath the truth, and how can either say with certainty that he hath it? We know not what is the truth. That we ourselves believe and feel absolutely certain that our own belief is true, is, in reality, not the slightest proof of the fact, seem it never so certain and incapable of doubt to us.

Therefore no man hath, or ever had, a right to persecute another for his belief; for there cannot be two antagonistic rights; and if one can persecute another because he himself is satisfied that the belief of that other is erroneous, the other has, for the same reason, equally as certain a right to persecute him.

The truth comes to us as the image of a rod comes to us through the water, bent and distorted: an argument sinks into and convinces the mind of one man, while from that of another it rebounds most quickly. It is no merit in a man to have a particular faith, excellent, and sound, and philosophic as it may be. It is no more a merit than his prejudices and his passions.

The sincere Moslem has as much right to persecute us, as we to persecute him; and therefore Masonry wisely requires no more than a belief in one great, all-powerful Deity, the Father and Preserver of the universe. Therefore she teaches her votaries that toleration is one of the chief duties of every good Mason. The Masonic system regards all the human race as members of one great family—as having the same origin and the same destination; all distinctions of rank, lineage, or nativity, are alike unknown. The whole tenor of the life of the benevolent Founder of the Christian religion was unremitting benevolence; His kind offices were extended alike to Gentiles and Jews, to publicans and sinners, as well as to His disciples.

Yet Masonry is eternally vigilant that no atheist or base libertine contaminates with his unhallowed tread the sanctum sanctorum of our temple; such can never gain admission there, without the grossest violation of vows the most sacred and solemn. It requires the acknowledgment of the existence of the Grand Master of the Universe, and to reverence his great and sacred name, irrespective of sectarian ideas; in a word, to practice every virtue which adorns and ennobles the human character, and fly every vice which sullies and degrades it. It inculcates a generous love for all mankind, it matters not of what religious creed.

No evil hath so afflicted the world as intolerance of religious opinion; the human beings it has slain in various ways, if once and together brought to life, would make a nation of people, which, left to live and increase, would have doubled the population of the civilized portion of the world; among which civilized portion it chiefly is that religious wars are waged.

No man truly obeys the Masonic law who merely tolerates those whose religious opinions are opposed to his own. Every man's opinions are his own private property, and the rights of all men to maintain each his own are perfectly equal. Merely to tolerate, to bear with an opposing opinion, is to assume it to be heretical, and assert the right to persecute, if we would, and claim our toleration as a merit.

The Mason's creed goes further than that; no man, it holds, has any right, in any way, to interfere with the religious belief of another. It holds that each man is absolutely sovereign as to his own belief, and that belief is a matter absolutely foreign to all who do not entertain the same belief; and that if there were any right of persecution at all, it would in all cases be a mutual right, because one party has the same right as the other to sit as judge in his own case—and God is the only magistrate that can rightfully decide between them.

To that Great Judge Masonry refers the matter; and, opening wide its portals, it invites to enter there, and live in peace and harmony, the Protestant, the Catholic, the Jew, the Moslem—every one who will lead a truly

NEGRO FREEMASONRY AND SEGREGATION

virtuous and moral life, love his brethren, minister to the sick and distressed, and believe in the One, All-Powerful, All-Wise, Everywhere-Present God—Architect, Creator, and Preserver of all things—by whose universal law of Harmony ever rolls on this universe: the great, vast, infinite circle of successive death and life; to whose ineffable name let all true Masons pay profoundest homage! for whose thousand blessings poured upon us let us feel the sincerest gratitude, now, henceforth, and forever. Amen.

(From: A Brief Account of the Scottish Rite, compiled by. H. A. Crosby, Milwaukee, 1911.)

A SELECTED BIBLIOGRAPHY

Baird, George W.; NEGRO MASONRY.

Benderson, William H.; A NARRATIVE HISTORY OF THE NATIONAL GRAND LODGE. (In Defense of the National Compact.)

Brent, Willis N.; COLORADO MASONS AND THEIR OPPONENTS.

Barthelmess, Richard; THE LODGES OF THE COLORED.

Caldwell, John D.; ST. ANDREW'S LODGE OF BOSTON.

Caldwell, John D.; NEW DAY—NEW DUTY.

Carson, Enoch T.; THE GRAND ORIENT AND NEGRO MASONRY.

Clark, Samuel W.; THE NATIONAL GRAND LODGE.

Clark, Samuel W.; THE NEGRO MASON IN EQUITY.

Crawford, George W.; THE ABC's of COLORED MASONRY.

Crawford, George W.; PRINCE HALL AND HIS FOLLOWERS.

Darrah, Delmar D.; THE HISTORY AND EVOLUTION OF FREEMASONRY.

Davis, Harry E.; A HISTORY OF FREEMASONRY AMONG NEGROES IN AMERICA.

Davis, Harry E.; THE SCOTTISH RITE IN THE PRINCE HALL FRATERNITY.

Delaney, Martin R.; THE ORIGINS AND OBJECTS OF ANCIENT FREEMASONRY; ITS INTRO-

DUCTION INTO THE UNITED STATES AND THE LEGITIMACY AMONG COLORED MEN.

DIGEST OF SPURIOUS FREEMASONRY IN THE UNITED STATES. (Masonic Service Association.)

Ferguson, Charles; FIFTY MILLION BROTHERS.

Gould, Robert Freke (Editor); CONCISE HISTORY OF FREEMASONRY.

Grimshaw, Harry A.; HISTORY OF FREEMASONRY AMONG THE COLORED PEOPLES OF NORTH AMERICA.

Hayden, Lewis; MASONRY AMONG C O L O R E D MEN IN MASSACHUSETTS.

Haywood, Harry LeRoy & Craig, Jas. E.; A HISTORY OF FREEMASONRY.

Johnson, Melvin M.; BEGINNINGS OF FREEMASONRY IN AMERICA.

Mackey, Albert G.; ENCYCLOPEDIA OF FREEMASONRY.

Norton, Jacob; REVOLUTION AND ASSUMPTION.

Parham, Wm. H. & Brown, Jeremiah A.; HISTORY OF THE GRAND LODGE, F. & A. M., OHIO.

Pitts, A. G.; PRECEPT VS. PRACTICE.

Robbins, Sir Alfred; ENGLISH SPEAKING FREEMASONRY.

Robbins, Joseph; NEGRO MASONRY.

Ross, Peter; HISTORY OF FREEMASONRY IN NEW YORK.

Shepherd, Silas H.; ESSAY ON MASONIC HISTORY.
Sibley, W. S.; THE STORY OF FREEMASONRY.
Stewart, L. C.; NEGRO FREEMASONRY OF TO-DAY.
Stillson, Henry L.; HISTORY OF FREEMASONRY AND CONCORDANT ORDERS.
Tatsch, J. Hugo; FREEMASONRY IN THE THIRTEEN COLONIES.
Thornburgh, George; HISTORY OF FREEMASONRY.
Upton, William H.; LIGHT ON A DARK SUBJECT.
Upton, William H.; NEGRO FREEMASONRY.
Upton, William H.; PRINCE HALL'S LETTER BOOK.
Voorhis, Harold Van Buren; NEGRO FREEMASONRY IN THE UNITED STATES.
Washington, Booker T.; THE STORY OF THE NEGRO.
Williamson, Harry A.; FREEMASONRY AMONG AMERICAN NEGROES.
Williamson, Harry A.; A PRINCE HALL PRIMER.
Williamson, Harry A.; NEGROES AND FREEMASONRY.